Sunset

Tax$aver
Homeowners

By Jay Knepp, CPA
Tax Specialist

Lane Publishing Co. ■ Menlo Park, California

Edited by Fran Feldman
Coordinating Editor: Linda Selden
Design: Brooklyn Graphic
Cover Design: Design Systems Group

Sunset Books
  Editor: David E. Clark
  Managing Editor: Elizabeth L. Hogan

First printing January 1987

From Coopers & Lybrand

We have reviewed *Homeowners Tax$aver* for accuracy in its description of federal income tax law.

Based on our interpretation of the Internal Revenue Code (including 1986 amendments) and its regulations, public rulings, and court decisions, we believe that *Tax$aver* accurately describes and interprets the applicable provisions of the law. Any taxpayer who follows the guidance of *Tax$aver* will have appropriate documentation to support his or her home-related deductions.

However, it is important to recognize that federal income tax laws and application of the Internal Revenue Service code and regulations are often a matter of interpretation. As a result, an Internal Revenue Service agent examining a taxpayer's return may disagree with the treatment of certain items of income and deductions as covered in this book. Because tax laws are continually subject to change by legislation, Internal Revenue Service regulations, public rulings, and court decisions, we cannot guarantee that a position taken by a taxpayer based on information in this book will not be successfully challenged by the Internal Revenue Service. In addition, individual facts and circumstances may result in an outcome different from that anticipated.

In view of the complexities of the tax laws and varying interpretations, taxpayers should not rely solely on the advice contained in *Tax$aver*, but should use it in conjunction with advice from their own tax advisor.

(Coopers & Lybrand is an international accounting firm with 98 offices in the United States.)

Table of Contents

Contents (Cont'd.)

Logs & Registers

Tax Help

Index

If you're a homeowner or you're considering buying a home and want to learn more about its income tax benefits, then *Homeowners Tax$aver* is for you. It's a unique combination of tax advice and information plus a systematic record-keeping system designed to give the IRS the records it demands—and, in some cases, even more.

This book, specifically created with the homeowner in mind, is designed for *you*, not for a tax specialist. It contains complete tax information on the situations (personal, business, or investment) you might encounter as a homeowner and tells you what you can deduct, how to keep required records easily and simply, and how to prove your claims should you be audited. Changes resulting from the passage of the Tax Reform Act of 1986 are highlighted in the text.

Above all, this book will help you minimize your taxes by showing you how to claim each and every deduction you deserve—the goal of all taxpayers.

Deductible Homeowner Expenses

Virtually all homeowners are aware of annual deductions you can claim for interest on your mortgage and for real estate taxes. But you may also be able to deduct other expenses that you incur as a homeowner.

Buying a home. Deductions are available in the year you purchase your home; other costs are added to your purchase price, which then becomes your original cost basis in the property. Knowing your home's basis, the amount of your ongoing investment, is especially important when you sell your home at a later time. This book will help you determine your current basis (called adjusted basis) and will allow you to keep an accurate accounting of it over time.

If the home you're buying is a second or vacation home, you'll need to be aware of the deductions and special rules that apply, especially if you plan to rent it out occasionally.

Deductions while you own your home. During the years you own your home, you can incur any number of deductible expenses. Using part of your home as an office is one example. Another is when you store inventory in your home or operate a day-care facility there. Even the use of a personal computer in your home for business purposes can lead to new deductions. The same is true if you entertain for business in your home.

If you're unfortunate enough to experience a loss due to a theft or catastrophic event, such as a fire or flood, you'll need to know what action you can take to minimize the effect of any financial loss.

Selling and buying another home. Each year, millions of taxpayers sell and/or replace their home. Because significant dollar amounts are involved, careful tax planning ahead of time is crucial. You must commit to making an additional investment of time to maintain records that will survive IRS scrutiny.

You'll learn what you must do either to reduce a taxable gain or to postpone or exclude all or part of it. And in the rare instance that your property is condemned for public use, you'll know what some of your options are *before* it's too late to react.

And since selling your home means you'll have to move, we outline all the moving expenses—and there are many—that are deductible.

The Importance of Good Records

Good records will help you prove not only the amount and type but also the nature of each expenditure, essential for determining whether or not it's a valid deduction. With this book, you'll be armed not only with knowledge but also with excellent records for your home-related deductions. Together with receipts and other evidence, these records will help you substantiate all your claims.

Permanent annual records. The tax information and forms included in this book are designed for one year's use. The reasons for this are simple and logical. Tax laws change constantly and starting a new book each year enables you to keep up to date with changes in tax law, as well as current developments. It reduces the chance you'll waste time and energy keeping records that are no longer required, or fail to meet some new requirement, which could prove costly. Also, with a permanent annual record, you'll always be prepared in the event the IRS questions your return.

Keeping abreast of tax law. Laws and regulations pertaining to homeowners change rapidly and often. In addition, court decisions are continually influencing and reinterpreting tax law. Because many areas in tax law are simply too complex for the average taxpayer, it's always wise to consult a competent professional tax advisor about any situation that concerns you, especially where large amounts of money are involved. For this reason, we've included a section to help you choose a competent professional tax advisor.

Tax terms. Baffled by the complicated terms used by the IRS in their tax forms and publications? In order to comply with all the regulations, it's essential to understand and speak their language. For definitions of the most commonly used terms, consult the glossary beginning on page 140. ◼

Record-Keeping & Substantiation Requirements

Whether you're preparing your own tax return, turning your records over to a professional tax advisor, or facing an audit by the IRS, complete tax records maintained in an orderly, organized fashion are essential.

Clearly, if you want to deduct any expenses related to home ownership and thereby reduce your tax bill, you're going to have to maintain records that substantiate your claims. It's no secret that many taxpayers regard this work as tedious and unpleasant. But once you know what constitutes good records and how to keep them, and you understand how to use the specially designed forms in this book, you can claim your deductions with ease and confidence.

What are adequate records? The IRS does not require you to keep records in any particular form or by any special method. They say only that you must have adequate records and sufficient evidence which, in combination, can prove the amounts shown on your return as income, deductions, and credits. When these amounts relate to business travel and entertainment expenses, you'll have to prove for each separate expense the amount, date, place, and business purpose.

Receipts are ordinarily the best evidence to prove the *amount* of an expense. You can prove the *time* element by recording the date of each expenditure or business use of an asset. The *place* element can be proven by indicating where the entertainment or business use occurred. Document the *business purpose* by recording the business reason for the expense or the nature of the benefit gained or expected. (Unless the business purpose of an expense is clear from the surrounding circumstances, a written statement is generally required.)

Entertainment expenses require a fifth element of proof—*business relationship*. You need to show the name, title, company name, or some other designation sufficient to establish the business relationship to you.

These records should be permanent, accurate, complete, and supported by any documents that clearly establish the nature and intent of each expense. Remember, however, that any record or evidence is not the sole determinant of deductibility. The facts and circumstances of each case will often dictate the final tax result.

How elaborate your records are depends on your individual situation. However, canceled checks or entries on a desk calendar alone are not usually considered as proper proof when unsupported by other documentary evidence.

When to make entries. The IRS is emphatic that records written at or near the time the expense occurs and supported by sufficient documentary evidence are much more credible than evidence reconstructed later. However, log entries do *not* have to be contemporaneous.

According to current IRS regulations, entries for automobile and other business expenses made on a weekly basis are acceptable. What this means is that you can accumulate your receipts and notes and make all entries on the appropriate forms once a week.

How to keep good records. This book provides all the specific instructions and forms you'll need for deducting expenses of home ownership. Since your records will have the highest degree of credibility if maintained close to the time the use or expense occurs, decide on when it's most suitable for you to make entries and develop a routine. Don't rely on memory—it's easy to forget the amount or reason for incidental expenses, which can add up quickly.

Tax$aver Tip. *An excellent way to keep track of all deductible expenses, regardless of how paid, is to use a portable tape recorder. That way, you can tape-record all your activities and expenses during the week, then write down the information the following week. It's a good idea to initial and date the entry.*

Here are some additional hints which may be of help:

- Always pay by check or credit card if possible, since you're instantly creating a useful record.
- Always ask for a receipt, especially when paying cash, and keep all receipts on file.
- When you can't get a receipt for a cash payment, record and explain the payment in your records as soon as possible.
- Though most expenses should be recorded separately, incidental expenses can be totaled by categories; for these you can make *one* entry for the entire day.

How long to retain records. All logs, checkbooks, canceled checks, receipts, and tax returns should be retained for at least 3 years from the date of filing, the usual length of time the IRS may select a return for audit. However, if it's found that some income was not reported and it's greater than 25% of what was reported, the period available for audit is 6 years after the return was filed. And the IRS can go back to *any* year when no return is filed, a return is false or fraudulent, or criminal activity is suspected.

The following records should be retained indefinitely:

1. Records that pertain to income-averaging when you need the information for the base period years (repealed, effective in 1987)
2. Records that relate to the basis of property subject to depreciation and that are needed to figure the gain or loss on sale of the asset, or the basis of new property when a trade-in is involved
3. Business or investment property records required to figure the amount of depreciation or investment tax credit recapture due to sale or disposition of the property before the end of its estimated recovery period

You'll also need records from prior years if you file a claim for a refund for taxes you've overpaid, if you need to amend a prior year's return, or if changes in tax law entitle you to benefits only on the basis of previous years' records. Often, records can also be helpful to the executor of your estate.

If a prior year's return is lost or misplaced, you can get a copy from the IRS. Ask for Form 4506—Request for Copy of Tax Form.

Lastly, secure all records relating to a specific tax year in an envelope and store it in a safe place. Think of these records as tax insurance.

Penalties for understatement of tax liability. Whenever noncompliance with the tax laws results in an underpayment of tax due to negligence or intentional disregard of rules and regulations, you're subject to a penalty equal to 5% of the amount of the deficiency related to negligence, interest, and an additional penalty equal to 50% of the interest due on the underpayment. Under the provisions of the Tax Reform Act of 1986, the penalty for substantial understatement of tax liability is 25% of the amount of the understatement, and the penalty for any amount attributable to fraud is 75% of the amount of the deficiency related to fraud. ■

Buying & Improving Your Home

If you need to compute depreciation on property converted to business or rental use, if you suffer a casualty or theft loss, or if you sell your home, you have to know the property's original cost, called *basis,* and any changes in basis over the years, called *adjusted basis.* The discussion that follows explains how to determine both amounts.

A form for summarizing changes in basis from year to year is on page 84.

Original basis. For most homes, original basis is the purchase price of the property, which includes your cash down payment plus new or assumed mortgage loans and any notes you gave to the seller.

If your home was built on land you owned, start with the adjusted basis of the land; then add all directly related costs incurred to complete construction, such as payments to contractors, costs of labor and materials, sales tax, interest and taxes during construction (may be deductible at your option), equipment rental, architect's fees, and utility meter and connection charges. If you built all or a portion of your home yourself, exclude from basis the value of your labor and any other labor you didn't pay for.

Settlement fees and *closing costs* charged to you in connection with a mortgage loan are added to basis, currently deductible, or neither.

The following are added to basis:

- Abstract and appraisal fees of the lender
- Amounts that are the seller's liability, but which you agree to pay
- Costs of defending or perfecting a title
- Costs of preparing loan documents
- Legal and recording fees
- Points not deductible because they're a charge for specific services (such as on VA and FHA loans)
- Purchase commissions and finder's fees
- Settlement and notary fees
- Surveys and transfer taxes
- Title insurance

If you're depreciating the property for business or rental income reasons, you'll need to divide the basis between the land and the building. Base your allocation either on the lender's appraisal (if land is shown separately) or on the most recent property tax bill.

Basis other than cost. If you've acquired property in a manner other than purchase, you can't use cost as the original basis. Often, you'll need to determine the property's fair market value (FMV), the amount a willing seller and buyer would accept, with reasonable knowledge of the facts and under no undue pressure to buy or sell. An appraisal by a competent professional and sales of similar property around the same time are helpful in determining FMV.

Property acquired by gift has an adjusted basis (for the purpose of determining gain) that is the same as it would be in the hands of the donor or the last owner by whom it wasn't acquired by gift. For determining loss, however, the lesser of this amount or the FMV, both on the date of the gift, must be used as basis. The tax implications are complex, so consult your tax advisor.

Inherited property's basis generally is its FMV at the date of death of the decedent. But it can be later if, for federal estate tax valuation purposes, the alternate valuation date is chosen.

For *property acquired by trade* for other property, your original basis is the adjusted basis of the old property, plus any recognized gain or cash you paid or less any recognized loss or cash you received.

Adjusted basis. During the period of time you own real or personal property, its original basis can increase or decrease. The result of all those changes is called adjusted basis.

Increases to basis must be capitalized, that is, added to basis, except for interest and taxes during construction, which may be claimed as itemized deductions. The following are increases to basis:

- Capitalized value of a redeemable ground rent
- Carrying charges you must pay to own or develop property
- Demolition costs (added to basis of land)
- Energy conservation costs and renewable energy source costs, both net of claimed energy credits

- Investment tax credit recaptured (personal property only)
- Improvements and additions with a useful life of a year or more (see page 21)
- Legal fees for obtaining a decrease in a levied assessment against property
- Refinancing closing costs (certain ones only)
- Repairs if included in extensive remodeling or restoration after a casualty
- Special assessments for local benefits and other nondeductible taxes (see page 31)

Decreases to basis—any items that actually or in effect represent a return of your investment—include the following:

- Amounts considered as unstated interest
- Casualty and theft loss deductions, which reduce basis by the amount of insurance proceeds or any other reimbursements, as well as by any deductible loss not covered by insurance (see page 55)
- Depreciation, which reduces the basis of business or rental property only by the amount claimed or that should have been claimed with one exception: when the deduction limitation rules for home offices, rental property, and hobby ventures result in some of the depreciation being disallowed solely because of the limitation (see pages 35 and 49)
- Easements or rights-of-way granted; the amount received is considered as a sale of an interest in your property. The basis of any portion that's retained is reduced by a pro rata allocation of the proceeds; if the amount received exceeds the basis, the basis is reduced to zero with the excess recognized as gain.
- Canceled debt only if omitted from income
- Condemnations, net severance damages (see page 67)
- Deductions previously allowed (or allowable) for amortization, depletion, or obsolescence (business or investment property only)
- Energy credits claimed if not deducted from cost of energy items added to basis
- Investment tax credit on certain historic and rehabilitated buildings
- Involuntary conversions resulting in recognized losses (see page 67)
- Postponed gain from the sale of a former residence (see page 62), which reduces the basis of your new home by the amount of gain not recognized on the sale

15

- Real estate taxes that are your liability but that are paid by the seller

Tax$aver Tip. *If you've owned your home for many years and haven't kept track of changes to basis, try to reconstruct them in order to arrive at adjusted basis at the beginning of the current year.*

To determine the cost of your improvements, review your records or ask your contractor or perhaps even the store where you purchased materials and supplies if they have any records. If necessary, have an appraiser estimate the cost of the improvements. Though you won't save any immediate tax dollars, you will when you sell your home.

Spousal transfer of property. When property is transferred between spouses or to former spouses and if incident to a divorce, tax law allows for no recognition of gain or loss to the spouse who transferred the property. Records necessary to determine adjusted basis of the property as of the date of transfer must be supplied to the spouse receiving the property. Further, a statement and signed election by both parties must be attached to the first income tax return filed by the spouse who transferred the property. ■

When you buy a home, you and the seller will agree to divide certain expenses resulting from your purchase. This section deals only with those expenses you can deduct (if you itemize) in the year you bought the home. Other costs of buying a home (those that are either nondeductible or added to basis) and the ongoing expenses of home ownership are covered elsewhere.

Expenses you can deduct will appear on your settlement or closing statement. It will show all charges and credits that occurred during the time it took the financial institutions to finalize the transaction.

Tax$aver Tip. *Make a copy of the statement and keep the original in a safe place. It will be invaluable in proving the original cost basis of your home, which you'll need to know when the home is sold.*

Interest. As the buyer, you're liable for interest on the mortgage beginning with the date of sale. If your closing statement shows interest allocated to you, record it in the register beginning on page 86 so you'll be sure to deduct it.

Tax$aver Tip. *If you're building a home, don't forget to deduct interest charged during the period of construction. This deduction is allowable only if the property isn't expected to be used in a trade or business or in an activity conducted for profit.*

When you buy a home late in the year and your closing statement has an interest charge that applies to the following year, it must be deducted in that year, not in the year paid.

Points paid by borrower. Points is a term used to describe such charges as loan origination fees,

17

maximum loan charges, or premium charges paid by the borrower, and basically amounts to an adjustment of the stated interest rate earned at the beginning of the loan. Points can be deducted as interest *only* if the charge is for the use of money, not a charge for a specific service. In most cases, points are treated the same as prepaid interest and are deducted pro rata over the term of the mortgage.

However, there's a key exception to this rule that applies to many home buyers. If the following conditions are met, you can deduct the entire amount paid as points in the year paid:

1. Your loan is to buy or improve your principal residence and is secured by that residence.
2. The payment of points is an established business practice in the area where the loan is made.
3. The points paid are generally the same as charged by others in this area.
4. The points are paid from separate funds you have, rather than being added to the loan balance.

If you paid more than what is generally charged, you're required to treat the excess as prepaid interest and deduct it over the life of the loan.

Tax$aver Tip. *To secure your deduction for points, ask the financial institution to clearly establish the amount of points related to use of money and those charges that are for specific services.*

Also ask for a letter verifying that paying points is an established business practice in the area and that the amounts are generally the same as those charged by others in that area.

Taxes. When real property is sold, real estate taxes must be prorated between the seller and buyer according to the number of days each owned the property. It also doesn't matter whom the tax is imposed on or who pays it. The closing statement should show that the seller was allocated an amount for the days up to, but not including, the date of sale; the buyer's allocation begins on the day of the sale. The person liable for the tax must deduct his or her allocable share *only* in the year actually paid.

Tax$aver Tip. *If the seller is legally liable for the tax, you as the buyer can choose between deducting your allocated share in the year of sale or in the year of actual payment, whichever is best for you.*

Normally, any real estate taxes paid during periods of construction are deductible, unless the property is to be used for business or investment purposes. If so, they must be added to basis and, under the Tax Reform Act of 1986, must be depreciated over the life of the asset. ■

If the sale of real property occurs before the current tax has even been determined, the title company must estimate the amount, based on the preceding tax bill or some other factor, and allocate it between buyer and seller. If the actual amount paid later is greater than the estimate, the buyer deducts the allocable portion of the actual payment with the excess added to basis.

Tax$aver Tip. *Remember that any taxes you pay for any year that are not deductible for any reason should always be added to basis.*

Leasing a Home with an Option to Buy

An agreement to lease with an option to buy usually occurs when a prospective buyer doesn't have the necessary down payment and/or can't arrange for long-term financing. By making an agreement with the seller/owner of the property, the tenant can, in effect, buy time in order to arrange such financing.

Writing the agreement. The parties involved should decide on a maximum time period and whether to include an option to renew. Other negotiable points are as follows:

1. Will there be a lump-sum advance option payment applied to the purchase price if the option is exercised? If it's not exercised, is the payment refundable? Can the payments be made quarterly or semiannually?
2. Is the eventual selling price a fixed amount or is it negotiable?
3. Will any portion of interim rent or any deposits be applied against the purchase price?
4. Who's responsible for insurance and repairs during the option period?
5. Can the tenant sell the option to someone else during or at the end of the period?

There are risks involved in such an agreement for both parties. The tenant could lose all payments made if financing can't be arranged by the due date. The owner defers receiving proceeds from the sale and could even lose money if the property's value increases above the fixed sales price.

Tax effects. If you're unable to make the purchase at the end of the period, there's no deductible loss, since all payments are of a personal nature. If you exercise the option, you won't have any deductions (except for deductible closing costs), but all payments applied to the purchase price per the agreement become part of the property's original basis. If you sell the option at a profit, it's a capital gain. (Note that in 1987 the maximum capital gains rate increases from 20% to 28%; beginning in 1988, the rate is the same as on other income.) If the option is sold at a loss, it's nondeductible. ■

Virtually everyone who buys a home will spend money to improve it at one time or another. Whether those expenses are major or minor, it's very important that they be added to the property's basis (see page 14). Though the expenditures can't be deducted, they can reduce any gain you might realize when you eventually sell the property.

There's now another reason to know and be able to prove the cost of your improvements. Under the Tax Reform Act of 1986, the amount of deductible interest on a mortgage incurred after August 16, 1986, is limited to the purchase price of the home *plus* the costs of improvements made since you bought your home. Interest on a loan in excess of that amount is certain to be deductible *only* if the proceeds are used for medical or educational expenses, or for improvements to that property. (See page 23 for more information.)

What is an improvement? The IRS says that an improvement must either materially increase the value of the property or extend its useful life more than a year. It can also adapt the property to a new use, such as converting a basement into a recreation room. Using the form on page 84, record all improvements made to your property since the date of acquisition. Keep track of current improvements in the log on page 85. Be sure to include all costs, including amounts borrowed, for the following:

- Materials and supplies
- Freight and installation
- Labor (not your own)
- Equipment rental
- Payments to contractors or subcontractors
- Legal, architectural, survey, and appraisal fees
- Related travel and telephone expenses
- Building permits
- State or local assessments for improvements

Repairs. Sometimes, distinguishing between an improvement and a repair is difficult. Repairs or maintenance costs are *not* added to basis and are

21

not deductible unless incurred for business or rental purposes. Repairs simply preserve your home in normal operating condition without changing the purpose for which it was acquired. Repairs also don't extend its useful life or add to its value, as do improvements. Typical repairs include patching plaster, replacing window panes, and fixing anything that's broken.

> **Tax$aver Tip.** *When repairs are done as part of an extensive remodeling or restoration plan, the entire job is considered as an improvement, and the full amount can be added to basis.*

Allowable expenditures. Here's a brief list of expenditures that have been classified as improvements:

1. Additions: Decks, patios, garages, bathrooms, tennis courts, swimming pools, spas, air conditioning systems
2. Remodels: Bathrooms, kitchens, cabinets, skylights, fireplaces
3. Replacements: Furnaces, roofs, fences, wiring, plumbing
4. Other: Landscaping, driveways, walkways ■

If you have an adjustable rate mortgage (ARM) and fear that interest rates will rise in the future or if you have a conventional mortgage with a very high rate of interest, you may want to consider refinancing your loan. It may lower your monthly payments as well as significantly reduce the total interest paid over the life of the loan. Though the interest deduction you can claim on your return will decrease, the lower tax rates and increased standard deduction available under the Tax Reform Act of 1986 make that deduction less valuable compared with the savings of actual dollars over the years.

Deduction limitations. The 1986 tax law has established certain strict limitations on refinancing (including a credit line secured by your home) after August 16, 1986:

1. You can only deduct interest in full on a loan that's equal to the purchase price of your home *plus* the costs of any improvements you've made to that home.

2. Interest on a loan in excess of that amount will be certain to be deductible *only* if the proceeds are used for medical or educational expenses incurred close to the time of the loan or for improvements to that property.

Excluded from medical expenses are insurance payments for medical care. Educational payments include amounts paid for tuition, books, and away-from-home living expenses at all educational levels.

If you refinanced *before* August 17 and the debt exceeds your cost basis, that amount becomes your new cost basis for purposes of the above limitations. Under the rules, your basis should not take into account postponed gain from the sale of a former home, an involuntary conversion, or depreciation claimed.

Be aware that the interest expense deduction rules are different for Alternative Minimum Tax (AMT) computation purposes. If you think you may be subject to AMT, you'll need to consult your tax advisor.

Tax$aver Tip. *If you can meet the limitations and have sufficient equity, you can refinance your home or obtain a secured line of credit and use the proceeds to pay off consumer loans, since the interest deduction for them is being phased out, beginning in 1987.*

Costs of refinancing. Shop around for the best rates. Settlement fees and closing costs can be deductible, nondeductible, or added to basis. Generally, points paid for a refinanced loan are not deductible; usually, they're deducted pro rata over the life of the loan, regardless of how or when they're paid. For an exception to this rule, see page 18.

Tax$aver Tip. *If the points paid are typical for your area, you may deduct them in full only if all the proceeds are used to improve your principal residence and if your new loan is secured by that residence. If only a*

portion is used for improvements, deduct a pro rata portion (the old loan balance plus that portion) and treat the balance of the points as prepaid interest (see page 29), which must be deducted pro rata over the life of the loan.

You may be able to avoid paying cash for points and closing costs by adding them to the loan balance in exchange for a higher interest rate. In this case, points must be deducted over the life of the loan. (Be sure this still saves you interest.) Similarly, your old loan may have a prepayment penalty that may have to be paid in cash (in which case it's deductible) or added to your new loan balance (in which case it's treated as prepaid interest). If you're refinancing with the same lender, ask that the prepayment penalty be waived.

Interest savings from refinancing. A general rule is that you may benefit from refinancing if the new rate is 2% lower than the old one and you plan to live in your home for at least 3 more years. If so, you should recoup your refinancing costs in about 2 years. To illustrate the potential savings, a $100,000 loan paid off in 30 years at 10% will save $53,800 in interest over a loan at 12%. Of course, this general rule will also be affected by the number of points you're required to pay to obtain the loan and by other closing costs.

Some borrowers are going a step further and are reducing the term of their new loans from 30 to 15 years, providing they can afford the increase in monthly payments.

Protect yourself by asking the lender to calculate the costs and interest savings; or buy a "mortgage payment table" book from an office supply store and do it yourself.

If you're refinancing with the original lender, ask if a substitution loan rate policy can be issued for title insurance in lieu of a new owner's policy; this could save as much as 70% of the fee. ■

Tax$aver Tips. *If you presently have an ARM and you think that interest rates have either stabilized or will decrease, consider keeping your ARM. Also remember that as long as the 2%/3-year rule mentioned above is satisfied, you can still save by refinancing even if you just bought your home or have refinanced it in the past.*

Deductions While You Own

Interest paid for the use of borrowed money to purchase residential property (even if it's a second or third mortgage) is deductible on Schedule A if you itemize your deductions or on Schedule E if it's related to various types of rental property. To be deductible, your interest payments must be due to an existing, valid, and enforceable obligation resulting from a true debtor-creditor relationship and must be paid by you during the tax year.

Under the Tax Reform Act of 1986, interest on mortgages secured either by your principal or second residence is deductible if the loans don't exceed the purchase price of your home plus the cost of any improvements you've made, or if the proceeds are used for improvements or for educational or medical purposes. If they exceed these amounts, the interest paid is subject to the consumer and investment interest limitation rules, and some portion may be nondeductible. Special rules apply to particular situations and to loans made before August 17, 1986, so see your tax advisor.

What is interest? Any amount specified in the loan agreement that can be definitely determined as the cost of borrowed money can be deducted; it's not necessary that interest be computed at a stated percentage rate. Even payments that are called something else, such as payments in lieu of interest, can be deducted as interest. Payments for interest to a family member are deductible only if there is intent by *both* parties that the debt is to be repaid and a bona fide obligation exists.

Determining home mortgage interest. To determine the amount of your annual interest payment, you can use the monthly statements some lending institutions send borrowers. Totaling the interest payments on the 12 statements for the year will give you your interest deduction. Or you can use Form 1098—Mortgage Interest Statement, sent to you by January 31 if you paid $600 or more during the previous year. The amount on the statement does not include points or other prepaid interest. For information on deducting points, see page 17.

Graduated payment mortgages. Such mortgages provide for monthly payments that increase annually for a fixed number of years and then remain the same thereafter. In the early years, the payments are even less than the interest owed, so the unpaid interest is simply added to the loan balance. Cash basis taxpayers can deduct the interest only if it's actually paid, not when added to principal.

Shared appreciation mortgages. In this type of mortgage, the lender allows you to pay a lower rate of fixed interest than the prevailing one. In return, the lender shares in any appreciation in value of the mortgaged property (usually a specified percentage of the appreciation). This amount is deductible as interest when paid to the lender.

> **Tax$aver Tip.** *If you're refinancing a graduated payment or shared appreciation mortgage, do it with a different lender; that way, the interest that's due can be deducted at the time the loan is refinanced.*

Reverse mortgage loans. When a lending institution pays you a loan in installments over a period of months or years, it's called a reverse mortgage loan. The loan, secured by a mortgage on your home, is based on the property's value. When the loan agreement provides that interest is to be added to the loan balance monthly, cash basis taxpayers again can deduct the interest only if they actually pay it, not when it's added to the loan.

Unstated interest. Taxpayers with mortgages at a very low stated interest rate or none at all may be able to deduct part of their monthly payments as interest in an amount referred to as unstated interest. Consult your tax advisor or ask the IRS for Publication 537: *Installment Sales.*

Mortgage interest credit. Certain states are authorized to issue mortgage credit certificates to certain low-income homeowners. The rate, which varies from 10% to 50%, is a direct credit against your state tax liability. Though the maximum credit is $2,000, any unused amount can be carried over to later years. If you receive such a credit, you must reduce your itemized interest deduction by the amount of credit claimed. Thus, if you paid $4,000 in mortgage interest and were entitled to a 30% credit of $1,200, your net interest deduction on Schedule A would be $2,800 ($4,000 less $1,200).

Mortgage prepayment penalties. Many mortgage agreements require you to pay a penalty if you pay off your loan early. Despite the general rule that penalties are not deductible, these payments are deductible as interest.

Ground rent agreements. Annual or periodic rental payments under a redeemable ground rent agreement are treated as interest paid on mortgage indebtedness and are deductible if certain conditions are met. See your tax advisor if this situation applies to you.

Any payments made to terminate the lease and acquire title to the property from the lessor are not ground rents and are nondeductible. Nor are payments made under a nonredeemable ground rent agreement. But if they're related to a trade or business or for income-producing rental property, they can be deducted as rent.

Prepaid interest. You cannot deduct any interest paid in advance that's not a charge for the use of borrowed money in the current year. Prepaid interest must be deducted in the tax year to which it applies.

If you're required to pay a bonus or premium to get a loan and you pay it in advance, it's deductible pro rata over the life of the loan. When the premium, interest, or discount is subtracted from the loan proceeds, such as with an FHA loan, the deduction is claimed on a pro rata basis only as payments are made. If you later pay off the loan in full, deduct the remaining interest in the year paid.

Other mortgage interest deductions. Your mortgage interest deduction can also include charges for late payments as long as the charges weren't for a specific lender service. And when you sell your home, you can deduct interest up to, but not including, the date of sale as indicated on the settlement statement.

Refunds of interest paid. Cash basis taxpayers who receive an interest refund in the same year the interest was paid simply report the refund as income on Form 1040 and deduct the interest in full on Schedule A.

If the refund received was for interest paid and deducted in a prior year, you may or may not have to include all or part of it in income in the current year. Exclude it entirely if it relates to a year in which you didn't itemize. If you did itemize that year, all or part of it may be income, depending on how much of a tax benefit you received from the payment. Ask your tax advisor to figure the amount includible in income.

Recording mortgage interest. Use the Deductible Expense Register that begins on page 86 to record your interest payments for the year. Be sure to note whether the payment was to a financial institution or to an individual. Report deductible points on a mortgage separately. ■

To be deductible, real property taxes must be levied by proper taxing authorities at a like rate against all property in the area over which they have jurisdiction and must be for the welfare of the general public. The tax must be imposed on *you*, and *you* must be legally obligated for its payment.

An exception is when another person has legal title and is assessed the tax and you own a beneficial interest in the property. If you pay the tax to protect your interest, the payment is deductible by you. Similarly, if there is more than one owner and all are equally responsible, the one who pays the entire tax may deduct the entire amount.

For information on allocating real estate taxes when property is sold, see page 66.

Escrow accounts. Most homeowners make monthly payments that include an estimate for real estate taxes and insurance due in the near future. These are placed in an escrow account and accumulate until the date payments must be made. Your deduction is based *only* on the amounts actually paid to the tax authorities. They or the lender will usually send you information at the end of the year as to the total paid on your behalf during the year.

Special assessments. Special assessments and so-called local benefit taxes that tend to increase the value and benefit specific properties aren't considered real estate taxes and are not deductible. Typical examples are construction and improvements for local streets, sidewalks, public parking facilities, and the like.

However, taxes assessed against local benefits *are* deductible if paid to meet repair or maintenance costs or interest charges related to the benefit. But the burden of proof as to how the allocation between deductible and nondeductible expenses was made rests with you. Even if some portion known to be local benefits is included in the taxes paid, no portion is deductible if no allocation can be made.

Tax$aver Tip. *Any taxes you pay that are not deductible for whatever reason can be treated as a sale expense or added to basis. When the property is sold, additions to basis will either reduce the gain on the sale or increase any loss.*

Deducting tax payments. For a tax to be deductible, it must actually be paid during the tax year, generally January through December. If you pay by cash, always get a dated receipt. If you pay by check, the date of payment is the day you personally deliver the check to the payee or when it's mailed.

Tax$aver Tip. *If you're paying a large deductible amount or it's subject to penalties, make sure your letter is postmarked by the applicable due date. An alternative is to certify or register it with the post office.*

Some institutions allow payments to be made over the phone either by credit card or by transfer of funds. In this case, the payment date is the date reported on the institution's statement to you. When calling in the payment, ask when it will be recorded on their records as a payment and take whatever action is necessary to secure the deduction. Credit card payments are treated as cash payments on the date charged, even though payment to the credit card company might occur in the following tax year.

If you contest a certain tax liability and pay it under protest, it's still deductible in the year of payment. But if you settle later for a lesser amount, the refund or credit may have to be included in income in the year of settlement.

Proving your deduction. Real estate taxes paid can be documented by receipted, dated tax bills or by statements sent to you by your lender or taxing authority. Monthly statements from the lender may show reductions to the escrow account when payment is made.

Record tax payments in the Deductible Expense Register beginning on page 86. ■

If you're a salaried employee who owns a business on the side, some special IRS rules may apply to you.

Special IRS rules. Regardless of how serious you may be about making a profit, the IRS can rule that your trade or business is a hobby if you can't show a profit, no matter how small, in at least 3 out of 5 consecutive tax years (2 out of 7 years for endeavors related to horses), starting in 1987. The burden of proving the IRS wrong is up to you. But once you produce a profit in any 3 years, the burden of proof shifts to the IRS. (Extensions of this time period may be possible; consult your tax advisor.)

Even if your business is found by the IRS to be a hobby, you can still deduct expenses, but starting in 1987 they can't exceed your *net*, not gross, income from that hobby and thus can't be used to offset income from other sources. Also, expenses allowed against gross income must be deducted in a prescribed sequence identical to the

order for deducting home office expenses (see page 79).

Proving your profit motive. According to IRS regulations, the following factors must be considered to determine if your activities are engaged in for profit. No single factor is determinative.

1. The *manner* in which you carry on the business—whether you legally file under a business name, whether you keep professional and accurate financial records, whether you keep a separate bank account, and whether you abandon unprofitable methods
2. Your *expertise* or that of your advisor and the research and consultation carried on
3. The *time* and *effort* you have expended, such as when you change occupations to start the business
4. Your *expectation* of profits or that assets used will appreciate in value and later be sold at a profit
5. The *success* you have had in the past in carrying on similar or dissimilar activities, or in

converting an unprofitable business into a profitable one

6. Your *history* of income or losses in this business and the reason for your losses, such as unforeseen circumstances or depressed industry conditions

7. The *amount* of occasional earned profits, if any, in relation to the amount of the investment

8. Your *financial status* and whether you have other income which is substantial

9. Any elements of *personal pleasure* or recreation involved, though all facts and circumstances will be considered

There are other steps you can take to show that you're serious, such as engaging in long-range planning, advertising and promoting your product or service, and obtaining insurance and all necessary permits for your business.

Tax advantages for your business. When you're in business, there are numerous opportunities to convert the business portion of such everyday expenses as utilities, telephone, and insurance into legitimate business deductions. Travel and entertainment expenses may also be necessary to promote your business. If you have an office at home, *all* your business mileage for that particular trade or business becomes deductible, since you have no commuting expenses—you live and work at the same location. Your tax advisor can assist you with other tax-saving ideas.

Tax$aver Tip. *Since the Tax Reform Act of 1986 generally lowers the maximum tax rate to 28% for individuals and to 34% for corporations, you can save taxes by setting up your business as a sole proprietorship or partnership. But if the limited liability aspect provided by incorporating is important to you, consider forming an S corporation. This type of legal entity allows profits to be taxed at individual income tax rates, yet provides limited liability for its owners.* ■

In order to claim home office deductions, you must use part of your home in a profit-seeking trade or business on a regular basis, and very specific tests must be met. Your expenses may or may not be reimbursed, and with few exceptions, the home office must be your principal place of business. The business, however, does not have to be your *principal* business; it can be any business in which you're engaged, even part-time.

The rules explained here also apply to using your home for the storage of inventory and for day care, with one exception (see page 37). And if you have a home computer used for business, you may be entitled to deductions whether or not you satisfy the home office rules.

Beginning in 1987, the deduction for home office use can't exceed your *net*, not gross, income from the business (see page 79 for information on the income limitations). Though a 1985 court case decided that these limits do *not* apply when employees lease a portion of their home to their employers, the Tax Reform Act of 1986 bars such a deduction.

Since the rules relating to deductible home office expenses are complex and constantly changing, see *Sunset's Home Office Tax$aver* or your tax advisor for additional information.

Basic Rules

First of all, for purposes of home office rules, what is a home? The IRS says a dwelling unit can be an apartment, boat, condominium, house, mobile home, or other similar property. An unattached garage, studio, barn, greenhouse, or any other structure on the property that relates to use as living accommodations is also included in this definition.

Who deducts home office expenses? Except for regular corporations, anyone who meets the rules and tests can qualify for these deductions, including trusts, estates, partnerships, and S corporations.

35

Self-employed people whose only office space is in their home will most likely be able to satisfy all the requirements. The same is true for *outside salespeople* who do selling away from their employer's place of business and perform only incidental duties there. However, if you're required to sell at your employer's business location on a regular basis, even if the time spent is not significant, you don't qualify as an outside salesperson.

In general, an *employee* who uses a home office has the most difficulty claiming a home office deduction. Even if every other test is met, no deductions will be allowed unless the office is maintained solely for the *convenience of your employer*, not your own convenience. It's not enough that the office be appropriate and helpful to your duties; it must be *required* by your employer and be reasonably related to the nature of your job.

Interestingly, the IRS has not clearly defined the term *convenience of employer*, but instead considers the facts and circumstances of each case. This gives you some latitude as to how you and your employer interpret this quasi-rule. Keep in mind that the courts have ruled that your

employer's principal place of business is not necessarily *your* principal place of business.

Tax$aver Tip. *Tax advisors generally agree that employees should obtain a written policy statement or even a board resolution clearly stating that an office at home is convenient for the employer, not for the employee.*

Investors have not been allowed to claim home office deductions unless the income-producing activity constitutes a trade or business, such as being a broker or dealer. Thus, the courts have denied deductions for people who manage investment portfolios, read financial reports and periodicals, and invest in securities.

The Use Tests

To claim a home office deduction, you must prove that your home office is used both exclusively and regularly for business purposes. In addition, you must also prove that it meets at least *one* of the following three tests:

1. It's your principal place of business.
2. It's a place to meet customers or clients.
3. It's a separate structure not attached to your home.

Exclusive use test. Though much has been written about this test, it simply means that whatever *space* in your home is specified as being used for your trade or business can't be used for *any other purpose* by you or any members of your family during the taxable year. If you use it for *both* business and personal purposes, you don't meet the test and your deductions will automatically be disallowed.

Where your home office is located is very important, should you be audited. Dens used to be a major concern of the IRS; in one of their examples, they said that if the den was also used for personal purposes, you could not claim any deductions for business use. But the code does not use the word *room*; thus, the courts have overruled the IRS and said that the business space doesn't have to be entirely separate.

IRS regulations now state that "the phrase 'a portion of the dwelling unit' refers to a room or other separately identifiable space; it is not necessary that the portion be marked off by a permanent partition."

Whatever space is used must relate directly to your trade or business, so be sure it doesn't contain any usable nonbusiness items. And if the space includes a home computer, move it to another room when you use it for personal purposes.

Exceptions to exclusive use test. When you use a home as a day-care facility (see page 41) or for storage of inventory (see page 43), you do *not* have to meet this test.

Regular use test. Once you satisfy the difficult exclusive use test, you must also prove that you use the space on a regular, continuing basis, not just incidentally or occasionally. But the regulations are vague, stating only that "the determination whether a taxpayer has used a portion of the dwelling unit for a particular purpose on a regular basis must be made in light of all the facts and circumstances." Your best protection is to record

37

the time spent in your home office on the form beginning on page 112.

Principal place of business test. This test, the first of the three specified tests mentioned earlier, says that the business space in your home must be used exclusively and regularly as the principal place of business for *any* trade or business you operate. The word *any* is important here because Treasury regulations say that "a taxpayer is deemed to have a principal place of business for each trade or business in which the taxpayer engages."

If you're engaged in only one trade or business but at more than one location, you must determine which location is the principal one. To make this determination, the IRS takes into account the following:

1. The portion of total income from the trade or business attributable to activities at each location
2. The amount of time spent in activities related to that business at each location
3. The facilities available to the taxpayer at each location for purposes of that business

Some courts have developed what is known as the focal point test, which states that the principal place of business is the location where income is produced or where goods and services are offered to clients or customers. Others argue that the focal point approach overemphasizes the location and that a major consideration should be the amount of time spent in the home office compared to other locations. Other factors to weigh are the importance of the business functions performed in the home, the business necessity of maintaining an office, and the costs to establish it.

The log of home office use beginning on page 112 will help you determine your principal place of business.

Place to meet with customers test. To meet this second test, the IRS says that the business space in your home must be "used exclusively and on a regular basis as a place of business in which patients, clients, or customers meet or deal with the taxpayer in the normal course of the taxpayer's business. Property is so used only if the patients, clients, or customers are physically present on the premises; conversations with the taxpayer by telephone do not constitute use of the premises by patients, clients, or customers."

The rules also say that the use by customers must be substantial and integral to the conduct of your business and that occasional meetings are insufficient to meet the test. The phrase "patients, clients, or customers" is not all-inclusive, but encompasses anyone with whom you customarily deal in business.

You can meet this test, yet still conduct business primarily at a location other than your home. Generally, the IRS says that dentists, doctors, lawyers, and accountants would fall under this rule. They also mention barbers, beauticians, and owners of small grocery stores. Additions to this list could include salespeople, claims adjustors, and insurance and real estate agents.

Use of a separate structure not attached to your home.

The last of the three tests is perhaps the easiest to meet. Examples of separate structures are a barn, cottage or guest house, detached garage, greenhouse, studio, and workshop. Any exclusive and regular business connection will satisfy this test.

Failure to Meet Home Office Tests

If you fail to meet the tests and your home doesn't qualify for storage of inventory or as a day-care facility, you'll be denied a deduction for direct and indirect expenses (see page 78). Remember, however, that you're only losing *those* deductions. You can still use your home for business or other income-producing purposes and deduct, with no restrictions, any ordinary and necessary business expenses.

Deductions for a Home Computer

If you use a home computer for both personal and business purposes, you must be able to document your business and personal use in order to arrive at your business use percentage (BUP). This figure determines how much of the equipment's cost you can deduct. Keep track of your computer use in the log beginning on page 112.

Computer deductions and the 50% test. Computer owners can choose between a Section 179 deduction or depreciating their equipment over time. Each year that you can prove your computer is

39

used more than 50% for business, you can continue to benefit from accelerated depreciation and suffer no recapture of investment tax credit or Section 179 expense previously claimed. See your tax advisor to find out what options are available to you.

Tax$aver Tip. *If you expect to meet the 50% test each year, your best bet is to claim Section 179. This allows you to write off up to $10,000 of the cost of your computer the first year it's placed in service. (Note, however, that your Section 179 expense can't exceed your taxable income from the business in which the computer is used.) Even if you never meet the test, you can always deduct depreciation on a straight-line, 5-year life adjusted for each year's BUP.*

Additional restrictions for employees. In order for an employee to deduct the business use of a home computer, leased or owned, the IRS says the use must be for the convenience of the employer and its purchase or lease required as a condition of employment. If possible, obtain a written statement from your employer.

Deducting software. You have three options for deducting software, but your choice must be consistent from year to year. If the purchase price is small (under $100, for example), you can deduct the entire cost in the first year. If the price is significant, deduct the cost over a 5-year estimated life or, if you can establish why this is necessary, over a shorter period.

Substantiation. On your tax return, you're required to answer some very specific questions about current deductions for a home computer, such as when it was first placed in service and what the current year's BUP is. You'll also be asked whether you have written evidence to support the BUP claimed. Good records will help ensure your deductions. ■

When your home, or any portion of it, is used on a regular basis in a business devoted to providing day care for children, for individuals aged 65 or over, or for those who are physically or mentally incapable of caring for themselves, you are entitled to deduct certain direct and indirect expenses (see page 78) related to such a business. The services you provide must be for compensation.

Operating such a facility in your home exempts you from the exclusive use test discussed on page 37, since it's normally not practical to separate the part of your home used for day care and not have it available for personal use.

Definition of day-care services. The IRS defines day care as services which are primarily custodial in nature and which, unlike foster care, are provided for only certain hours during the day. These services may include educational, developmental, or enrichment activities incidental to the primary custodial services. If the services performed in the home are primarily educational or instructional in nature, however, they don't qualify as day-care services. The determination of whether particular activities are incidental to the primary custodial services generally depends on the facts and circumstances of the case.

Educational instruction to children of nursery school age is considered incidental to the custodial services. The same is true of educational instruction to children of kindergarten age if the instruction is not in lieu of public instruction under a state compulsory education requirement. Enrichment instruction in arts and crafts to children, handicapped individuals, or the elderly is also ordinarily considered incidental to the custodial services.

The IRS requires that the owner or operator of the facility must have applied for, been granted, or be exempt from having a license or other such approval under any applicable state law. This requirement is not met if either the application has been rejected or the license revoked.

Beginning in 1987, the deduction for day-care services is limited to the amount by which the *net*, not gross, income from such services exceeds direct and indirect business expenses.

How to compute the day-care deduction. When you use part of your home for business and meet all the required tests, you simply prorate the business portion of your home as a percentage, multiply it by all indirect expenses, and add expenses deductible in full to arrive at your deduction for the year. However, with day-care facilities, you must make an additional *special* allocation based on time used for day care compared to time available for *all* purposes. To do this, use a formula based on a 365-day year, giving you 8,760 total hours.

Here's an example of how to make this special allocation: you use part of your home for day care 9 hours a day for 260 days a year (52 weeks × 5 days per week), making a total of 2,340 hours. Divide the total by 8,760 to arrive at 26.7%. Multiply this percentage by all the *direct* expenses of the area used for day care. Then, assume that the area you use for day care is 30% of the total area of your home. This means you can deduct 8.01% (26.7% × 30%) of your *indirect* expenses, such as depreciation, interest, real estate taxes, insurance, and the like.

Use the form on page 117 to compute your business time percentage and your expenses. ■

You are allowed to deduct certain ordinary and necessary expenses for any portion of your home that you use on a regular basis to store inventory and goods you sell at wholesale or retail in a trade or business. Included in the definition of "home" is any separate, freestanding structure close to the house, such as a garage, studio, or barn used for storage.

Such use of your home exempts you from the exclusive use test described on page 37.

Typically, this deduction is available to the self-employed and to outside salespeople.

Tests you must meet. The IRS regulations state that "the storage unit includes only the space actually used for storage; thus, if a taxpayer stores inventory in one portion of a basement, the storage unit includes only that portion even if the taxpayer makes no use of the rest of the basement." You can still use the remaining area for personal purposes.

In order to deduct expenses, you must meet *all* the following tests:

1. The inventory must be held for use in your *trade or business*.
2. Your trade or business must be the selling of a product at either *wholesale or retail*, which includes mail order.
3. Your home must be the *sole fixed location* of that trade or business. Thus, if you have a small retail store and, because of space limitations, must store inventory in your garage, there is no deduction.
4. The space used must be a *separately identifiable* section of your home and be suitable for storage.
5. The space must be used on a *regular basis*. Incidental or occasional use, even if exclusive, will not suffice. The rules do say, however, that use on a regular basis will be determined in light of all the facts and circumstances.

What you can deduct. Any expenses, such as repairs or maintenance, that relate directly to the space used can be deducted in full. Other expenses that benefit the entire home must be prorated, based on your business use percentage, as explained on page 77. If you buy shelving or storage cabinets, you'll probably have to depreciate them over their useful lives. Employees claim business expenses on Schedule A as a miscellaneous deduction, subject to the 2% of adjusted gross income floor.

Deductions that were disallowed. Here are several examples of storage of inventory deductions that were disallowed by the courts.

A judge tried to deduct expenses for space adjacent to a carport to store records from prior years and furniture used in his law practice and as an office for managing real estate. His deductions were denied for several reasons. The records and furniture were not considered inventory, the space was not used on a regular basis, and the judge was not involved with his law practice during the year in question.

A pharmacist who was also an officer of the corporation had a home office and also stored prescription drugs at his residence. No deduction was allowed since his home was not the drug company's sole fixed location.

Use of a room at his home by an attorney-employee for storage of files and his law library was found not deductible since he was not in a trade or business of selling products at wholesale or retail.

Documenting your storage deductions. Keep track of your expenses in the Deductible Expense Register beginning on page 86. In addition to keeping receipts, bills, statements, and other substantiation, you may want to take some photographs at various times during the year. Take an inventory count periodically and record goods received and shipped. These records will help you prove that the space was used on a regular basis.

Tax$aver Tip. *Keep in mind that it's possible to meet both the tests for a room used as an office and the storage space rules, resulting in a larger business use percentage and, of course, in a larger deduction.* ■

Whether the home is purchased primarily as an investment or not, many owners of vacation homes both use the home themselves and rent it out to others. The rules for the rental use of such homes are generally the same as for other rental property, except that your deductions may be limited depending on the number of days the home is rented to others and the number of days it's used by you or your family. A form to keep track of the property's use and the rent collected begins on page 120.

According to the IRS, a dwelling unit can be a house, apartment, boat, condominium, motor home, mobile home, or any portion thereof. At the minimum, the unit should include a kitchen, sanitary facilities, and a place to sleep.

Reporting of Income & Expenses Not Required

If you rent your property to others for less than 15 days during the tax year, you're not required to report any rental income; nor can you claim any rental expenses as deductions. However, you can deduct interest (see page 27), property taxes, and casualty and theft losses attributable to the home on Schedule A, but only if you itemize. Under this rule, there are no restrictions on how often you can use the property as a residence.

Reporting Required with Limitations

Often, owners of vacation homes use their home regularly, but also rent it out whenever they can. When it's used for personal purposes for more than 14 days *or* more than 10% of the total days it was rented out during the tax year, whichever is greater, your rental expense deductions cannot exceed your rental income and must be deducted in a prescribed sequence, identical to the order for deducting home office expenses explained on page 79. (A form for computing these limits on rental deductions is on page 123.)

Report all rental use income and expense items on Schedule E; on the form, you'll be asked how many days you used the property. Deduct the personal use portion *only* of interest, taxes, and any casualty and theft losses on Schedule A if you itemize.

A dwelling is considered to be used for personal purposes (even for part of a day) when it meets any of the following criteria:

1. It's used by any person for less than a fair rental charge (about the same as charged for similar accommodations in the same area).
2. It's used by any person under a reciprocal arrangement and regardless of whether there's a rental charge.
3. It's used for personal purposes by any person who owns an interest in it, unless it's rented as a principal residence under a shared equity financing agreement.
4. It's used for personal use by any person who owns an interest in it or by their family, unless it's used as a principal residence and a fair rent is paid.

Don't count as days of personal use any day or major part of a day you spent doing repairs or maintenance, or any time it's rented at a fair rent

and you're a guest of the tenant for a few days. Don't include in rented days any days when your home was merely *available* to rent. Remember also that each day of use can only be counted in one category.

Effect of not being used as a residence. When your personal use of the home during the tax year doesn't exceed the greater of 15 days or 10% of the total days it was rented at a fair rental value, you're considered as *not* having used the dwelling unit as a residence. Instead, it's presumed that your property is an investment with a profit-seeking motive.

This means that after allocating between personal and rental use, your rental expenses are deductible in full with no limitations. Should this result in an overall net loss, it can then be offset against nonrental income. However, the Tax Reform Act of 1986 generally limits such rental losses to $25,000 and phases out this benefit for certain high-income individuals. Also, to offset your rental loss against any type of income, you must *actively* participate in the rental activity, by managing the property yourself, for example, and own at least a 10% interest in the property. To deduct a rental loss, you must charge *all* tenants a fair market rate.

All items of income and expense are claimed on Schedule E, with the personal portion only of interest, property taxes, and casualty or theft losses deducted on Schedule A.

Proving your profit motive. If the IRS shows that the rental use is not an activity from which you expect to make a profit, they may attempt to invoke the hobby loss rules. The general rule, as revised by the new tax law, is that if your efforts result in a profit for 3 or more years in a period of 5 consecutive tax years, it's presumed to be for a profit.

Allocating vacation home expenses. Whenever you're required to report your rental income and expenses, you must allocate your total expenses for the year based on the amount of rental and personal use. Rental days are those when the property was rented at fair market value (FMV), even if you personally used your vacation home on one of those days.

Tax$aver Tip. *Though you may not be able to control the number of days your property will be rented, you should always be aware of the current total since you **can** control the days of personal use. This way, you may be able to manage the percentage in the way that's most desirable for you.*

To get your percentage for allocating expenses, the IRS says to divide the total number of days rented at FMV during the year by the total number of days the property was used for rental and personal use (called the Rental Personal Method). Apply this percentage against total expenses to arrive at the rental expenses you can offset against rental income.

A second method that can be used, but *only* for allocating interest and property taxes, has been found acceptable by the courts. Under that method (called Total Year), divide the days rented at FMV by 365, which results in a smaller percentage being applied to interest and taxes.

Tax$aver Tip. *Whenever the limitation on deduction rules applies, use the latter method to reduce the amount of interest and taxes allocated to rental use so you can deduct a larger amount of other rental expenses that might otherwise be disallowed. This will also give you a larger overall deduction, since interest and taxes, though partially disallowed on Schedule E, can be deducted on Schedule A for the remaining balance.*

If the limitation rules don't apply, use the IRS method; since all rental expenses will be deducted at their fully allocated amounts, your adjusted gross income will be reduced, allowing you a larger deduction for medical, casualty, theft, and employee business expenses. Also use this method when you don't have enough deductions to itemize, since you'll want to shift as much interest and taxes to Schedule E as possible.

The form on page 123 allows you to compare the dollar effect of the two methods. Use the one that will be most beneficial to you.

Other tax considerations. Furniture, appliances, and the home itself can be depreciated, subject to the limitation rules, usually under either the straight-line or accelerated depreciation method, except for a home placed in service after December 31, 1986. In this case, you must use straight-line.

For information on selling a home used for personal and rental purposes, see page 64.

Tax$aver Tip. *If your vacation home suffers a large casualty or theft loss, try to increase the number of rented days at FMV and reduce the personal-use days. The rental-use days will **not** be subject—as the personal portion is—to either the $100 floor or the 10% of AGI rule.* ■

This section deals with the permanent or occasional rental of a portion or all of your home, and the temporary rental of your new or former home while you're trying to sell your old one. Be aware that when you sell your home, there are certain negative tax consequences to having rented it. For information on selling a home, see page 62.

Renting a portion of your home. Whether you regularly or occasionally rent out part of your home, you'll need to record the income and expenses associated with this profit-seeking activity. Your deductions for rental expenses may be limited and must be divided the same way as for home office expenses (see page 77). Allocate the indirect expenses based on either the number of rented rooms or the percentage of square feet used for rental purposes. Be sure to prorate expenses for the number of months there actually was rental income.

Record income in the log on page 120 and indirect expenses in the Deductible Expense Register beginning on page 86. Use Schedule E to report rental income and expenses.

Converting your home to rental property. If you decide to permanently rent your former home, you won't be able to postpone gain if you later sell the property.

To determine the basis for depreciating your former home, use its adjusted basis or fair market value, both on the date the property was converted, whichever is less. (See page 14 for a discussion of adjusted basis.)

Temporary rental income. A valuable tax benefit to homeowners when they sell their homes is the postponement of recognizing gain on the sale. The rules described below are designed to protect this benefit in two situations: first, when you buy a new home, live in it, and temporarily rent out your former home before selling it; and second, when you buy a new home and temporarily rent it out until you can sell and move out of your old home. In both cases, all homes must be or have been your principal residence. Even if the rental is merely for convenience, you can still defer gain on the sale.

If the temporary rental period is less than 15 days during the tax year, you don't have to include rent received in gross income; but you can't deduct any rental expenses other than those normally deductible, such as real estate taxes, mortgage interest, and casualty and theft losses. If the temporary rental period is 15 days or more during the year, you must report the rental income, and your rental expenses are limited and deducted in a prescribed order. (The rules are the same as for home offices—see page 79.)

If you've listed your home with a real estate agent with the intention of renting or selling it and it's not rented, it's still considered as your principal home, not investment property, and gain, if any, can be deferred. The IRS has not determined how long the property can go unrented and gain still be postponed. What you'll want to avoid is having them treat it as income-producing property, which means any gain on the sale will be taxable and cannot be deferred. However, if you expect a loss on the sale, you may want to rent the home for a period of time, since a loss when sold would then be deductible.

A mere offer to rent without actually renting it is not enough to convert it to a deductible loss, even though depreciation deductions may be allowed. But if you're able to rent it, you may be able to convert this nondeductible loss into a deductible one. The rental period can't be short, and you should get a qualified appraisal at the time the property is converted to substantiate the fair market value at that time. ■

The term entertainment, broadly construed, covers any activity of a type generally considered to constitute entertainment, recreation, or amusement. Because entertaining at home for business or investment purposes is not a usual deduction and little is written about it, few taxpayers deduct it. What you need to know is that the IRS is only concerned that taxpayers meet the strict entertainment rules and tests—a business benefit should be expected or received and the atmosphere should be conducive to discussing business.

Basic rules. To ensure your deduction, your records need to show why entertaining at home is more effective and helpful than doing so elsewhere. Few would argue with the fact that a home is more conducive to discussing business than a restaurant. Geographical location, cost, and the available time of the parties can also be logical reasons for entertaining at home.

The Tax Reform Act of 1986 sets new limitations on business meal and entertainment deductions. Your allowable deduction is generally reduced to 80% of the total expenditure, and no deduction is allowed unless business was discussed either during or directly before or after the meal or entertainment.

For entertaining at home, as with all business expenses, you must prove all the required elements of the expense and also pass the ordinary and necessary and either the directly related or the associated with tests.

The *elements* of the expense which must be recorded and substantiated include the following:

1. The amount of each separate entertainment expense, including tips
2. The date, place, and type of entertainment, and when and where the business discussion took place, as well as its duration
3. The business purpose of the entertainment
4. The name, title, and occupation of the persons entertained, and who discussed business

Any business expense is *ordinary* if it's a common and accepted practice in a particular trade or business; to be *necessary,* it should be appropriate and helpful in the performance, promotion, or furtherance of a trade or business.

The *directly related* test can be satisfied only if all the following requirements are met:

1. You had *more* than a general expectation of producing income or any other benefit at some future date, other than goodwill (though income or benefit doesn't have to result from each event).
2. During the entertainment period, you actively engaged in a business meeting, discussion, negotiation, or transaction with the person(s) being entertained.
3. The principal purpose of the entertainment was business, though it's not essential that you devote the majority of time to business to satisfy this requirement.
4. The money spent was allocable to the person(s) with whom you engaged in the active conduct of business during the entertainment.

Another way of satisfying the directly related test is if the entertainment occurred in a clear business setting which directly furthered your business.

Entertainment expenses are also deductible when considered *associated with* the active con-

duct of your trade or business if you establish a clear business purpose for the entertainment and it either directly preceded or followed a substantial business discussion. Whether a business discussion is substantial or not depends on the facts and circumstances in each case. Usually, this requirement will be satisfied if you verify that the principal character or aspect of the combined activity was the active conduct of business.

Use the entertainment log on pages 124–127 to record all the necessary information.

Tax$aver Tip. *Though a business discussion or meeting will usually occur on the same day as the entertainment, it could take place a day apart, such as when someone arrives from out of town.*

Exception to entertainment rules. Another deductible use of your home not subject to the restrictions on entertainment expenses is a meeting of your employees, partners, stockholders, agents, or directors. Though the primary purpose of the meeting must be company business, minor social activities are permitted.

Entertaining for goodwill. A legitimate objective of any business is to create, foster, and keep business goodwill. Though there are restrictions on entertainment for purposes of generating goodwill, such expenses can't be disallowed for that reason alone. According to the IRS, goodwill expenses are deductible in the following cases:

1. In limited situations under the directly related rule where the entertainment occurs in a clear business setting
2. When associated with the active conduct of business and the entertainment directly precedes or follows a substantial or bona fide business discussion

Who you can entertain. IRS regulations state that the people you can reasonably expect to engage or deal with in your trade or business include customers, clients, suppliers, employees, agents, partners, and professional advisors, whether established or prospective.

The expenses of spouses are also deductible if it's impractical under the circumstances to entertain without them. You can deduct costs related to other family members only if they assist in a business manner or provide a service.

Strictly speaking, your own meal is deductible only as to the amount that exceeds what you would have ordinarily spent. But this rule actually only applies to abusive cases where a taxpayer tries to deduct a substantial part of personal living expenses. In practice, the IRS typically allows the full cost of all meals to be deducted.

What you can deduct. Basically, you can deduct all the *direct* costs of each entertainment event. These costs include food, beverages (even when nothing else is served), catering, music, waiters, invitations, and cleanup, among others. You can also host a testimonial dinner and deduct it as long as it's less than $400.

Deductions by an employee. To secure deductions for entertaining at home when you're not reimbursed, you'll need a statement from your employer that it's a condition of your employer, that it's for your employer's convenience, and that it's been taken into consideration in determining your salary.

Under the Tax Reform Act of 1986, employees claim these expenses on Schedule A as a miscellaneous deduction (and attach Form 2106). Also, remember that the new law permits you to deduct only 80% of your entertainment costs. If you're fully reimbursed for your expenses, your employer is subject to the 80% rule. You can deduct your expenses in full. Miscellaneous deductions, in total, must exceed 2% of adjusted gross income to be deductible.

Keep in mind that, with good records, you can deduct any job-related entertainment expenses that are necessary to do your job.

Deductions not allowed. The IRS and the courts have disallowed entertainment deductions for the following:

- Expenses that are lavish or extravagant or that are estimates or approximations
- Expenses that an employee doesn't ask the employer to reimburse or that an employer refuses to reimburse
- Expenses for entertaining large groups at home

- Meals or entertainment when you and your business associates take turns frequently in paying for the expenses
- Meal expenses where only the fact that food was provided was shown

Tax$aver Tip. *If you're audited, the IRS may compare the frequency of your business entertaining, as well as those in attendance, with your social entertaining. Though not required, you may want to keep records about the date, frequency, and attendance of purely social events.* ■

Casualty damages to your home from catastrophic or other similar events or thefts of property may be deductible. Questions then arise regarding the determination of the amount of the loss and whether the property was used for personal or business purposes, or both.

Generally, business losses are fully deductible, reduced only by any insurance or other reimbursements. However, personal casualty and theft losses are subject to certain reductions and limitations which, in effect, allow only *major* losses to be deductible. In addition, such losses can be claimed *only* if you itemize your deductions. A form for recording casualty or theft losses as they occur is on page 128.

Casualty Losses

The IRS defines a casualty as "the damage, destruction, or loss of property resulting from an identifiable event that is sudden, unexpected, or unusual. A sudden event is one that is swift, not gradual or progressive. An unexpected event is one that is ordinarily unanticipated and one that you do not intend. An unusual event is one that is not a day-to-day occurrence and one that is not typical of the activity in which you were engaged." Also included as a casualty is the government-ordered demolition or relocation of homes considered unsafe due to a disaster.

Business casualty losses. These losses are treated like any other business expense, in that they are fully deductible after reduction by the amount of insurance or other reimbursements received or expected. If the casualty loss involves property used only partially for business, the loss must be divided as if there were two separate occurrences. The limitation rules discussed below apply only to the nonbusiness portion of the loss.

Generally, a casualty loss amount is the lesser of either the property's adjusted basis at the time the loss occurred or the decrease in its fair market value from immediately before to immediately after the casualty. However, if the property is *completely* destroyed, the deductible loss is the adjusted basis less any salvage value or insurance proceeds or other compensation either received or sure to be recovered. The decline in market value is ignored.

Personal casualty losses. As with business losses, the amount of the loss is the value of the destroyed portion of the property or the adjusted basis, whichever is less, reduced by any insurance or other reimbursements received or expected. However, there are two other reductions you must make:

1. Each loss must be reduced by $100.
2. You must further reduce the combined amount of all losses, casualty and theft, by 10% of your adjusted gross income.

The remaining balance, after these reductions, is the amount you may claim on your return, but *only* if you itemize your deductions. These reductions do not apply if you had a casualty gain because reimbursements exceeded your losses.

Married taxpayers filing jointly are subject to only one $100 reduction for each casualty (or theft) loss on their return. But each of them is subject to that limitation if they file separate returns.

Disaster area losses. If your loss is a result of a disaster in an area the President declares eligible for federal assistance, you have an additional option. You can claim the loss either in the year it occurred or in the immediately *preceding* tax year. Consult your tax advisor to find out what's best for your particular situation.

Examples of deductible losses. For your reference, the following events have been allowed as deductions for property losses and damages:

- Accidents, if unavoidable
- Cleanup expenses
- Earthquakes, earthslides, avalanches, sudden sinking of land
- Explosions, bomb damage, fires, lightning, volcanic eruptions
- Hail, snow, ice storms, blizzards, dust storms, hurricanes, tornadoes, sudden wind damage, smog (if unusual, sudden, or severe)
- Sonic booms

- Vandalism, looting, riots
- Water rise (if sudden), floods, tidal waves

Examples of nondeductible losses. The IRS has not allowed the following as personal casualty losses:
- Cost of unsuccessful accident property damage claim
- Damage or destruction of landscape by a fungus, disease, insects, worms, etc.
- Drought
- Erosion, rust, paint oxidization
- Personal injury damages paid, attorney fees, court costs
- Pet damage to property
- Progressive deterioration of any type
- Termite or moth damage

Note that most of the above losses *are* deductible if related to business or investment property, either as a business casualty or as a business expense.

Losses from Theft

The IRS defines a theft as "the unlawful taking and removing of money or property with the intent to deprive the owner of it. It includes, but it is not limited to, larceny, robbery, and embezzlement. You need only show that the theft was illegal under the law of the state where it occurred, and that it was done with criminal intent."

With very few exceptions, property or money that merely disappears or is mislaid is not considered a theft.

When to deduct. Such losses are deductible only in the year of discovery, which may or may not be the year the theft actually took place. If the year of discovery is over and you haven't filed your return yet, don't claim the loss if you think the property will be recovered; deduct such a loss only when it's clear that recovery will not occur. Then you'll need to prove that you were the owner of the property, that it was actually stolen, when you first discovered the theft, and how you arrived at the dollar amount of the loss.

If any of your property is stolen, contact a law enforcement agency and your insurance company immediately after you discover the theft. For tax purposes, however, it's not required that the police actually investigate the theft.

Amount of loss. The cost of the property and its fair market value at the time of the theft must be determined. As a cost basis, use your original sales contract, purchase orders, sales receipt, or other written proof. Your loss is either the full fair market value or adjusted basis (original cost plus improvements and, for business property, less depreciation, even if not claimed), whichever is less. If you later recover your property, your loss is either the decline in value from the time it was stolen until the time recovered or the adjusted basis before the theft, whichever is less.

Each nonbusiness theft loss must be reduced first by any insurance or other reimbursements and second by $100. Then, combine your theft loss with any casualty losses and deduct 10% of your adjusted gross income. This is the net amount you can claim. These reductions do not apply if you had a casualty gain because reimbursements exceeded your losses.

If the property was used solely for business, it's not subject to the $100 reduction or the 10% of adjusted gross income reduction, but the total must be reduced by any reimbursements.

If, as is often the case, the property was used for both business and personal purposes, treat the theft as if there were two separate occurrences, applying the $100 and 10% rules only to the non-business portion of the loss.

Supporting Your Claim

As you might expect, there have been many court cases involving casualty and theft losses claimed by taxpayers. These cases clearly show that you must have extensive proof to support your claim.

To record personal or business losses, use the form provided. In addition, gather the following written information as soon as possible after the loss occurs:

1. A statement as to the nature and type of casualty, and how the loss was a direct result, with copies of any available insurance, fire, or police reports

2. Proof of ownership of the property or, if leased, that you were contractually liable for the damage

3. Sales contract, lease agreement, or other evidence supporting the purchase price; receipts

and canceled checks to support any major additions or improvements to the property

4. Appraisals, insurance adjustors' opinions, or reports showing how the fair market value before and after the casualty was determined (for accidents, this is usually a damage estimate by a qualified person)

5. Photographs showing the extent of damage

6. Receipts for any damage repairs completed

7. In a case of theft, a copy of the police report proving the theft and showing when you discovered the property missing

Tax$aver Tip. *The cost of an appraisal is deductible as a miscellaneous deduction on Schedule A if you itemize and regardless of whether or not the 10% limitation eliminates your casualty or theft loss. Starting in 1987, miscellaneous deductions are subject to a 2% of adjusted gross income floor.*

Many taxpayers do not file insurance claims for casualty and theft losses because they fear that their premiums may increase or that the policy may even be canceled. The Tax Reform Act of 1986 says that you are *not* allowed to claim a non-business casualty loss deduction if you haven't filed a timely insurance claim.

Tax$aver Tip. *It's important, and usually relatively easy, to prove the original purchase price of property. If you don't, the IRS may arbitrarily set the amount, which could reduce your loss dramatically. It's best to investigate all the acceptable methods of valuing your property both before and after the loss; you can then use the method that gives you the highest value.*

Adjustments to cost basis. All property, business or personal, has an ongoing measurement of investment, called basis, which usually is the original cost. Casualty and theft losses decrease your basis by the amount of the deductible loss and any insurance or other reimbursements received. Any money spent to repair or restore your property will increase the basis. And if your reimbursements are greater than the basis before the casualty, this excess gain is taxable and added back to basis.

How and where to report. To report casualty or theft losses, transfer the information on page 128 to Form 4684; use Section A for personal casualty and theft losses, Section B for business losses.

> **Tax$aver Tip.** *If the amounts claimed are large, attach complete documentation directly to your return to help avoid an audit.*

If your situation involves a wide range of gains and losses involving various types of property, if your insurance proceeds exceed the loss, or if you have a casualty or theft loss that exceeds your income, you may have to amend prior years' returns. In this event, it's best to consult your tax advisor to assure yourself of maximum tax benefits.

Publications 547, 549, and 584 are available from the IRS if you need more information. ■

Selling or Disposing of Your Home

Selling Your Home

For virtually all taxpayers, selling a home has major tax consequences. If you sell it at a gain, either you may have to pay tax on the gain or you may be able to temporarily postpone all or a portion of it from tax. If you're 55 or older and haven't previously utilized the benefit, up to $125,000 in gain can be *permanently* excluded from being taxed (see page 64).

If you incur a loss on the sale, only the portion of the loss attributable to the business use of your home (if any) is deductible.

To qualify for postponement or exclusion, the home sold and replaced must be your principal residence (not a second or vacation home).

Postponing recognizing gain. Generally, when you sell your residence at a profit and, within 2 years before or after the sale, buy another that costs as least as much as what you sold your old one for, you *must* postpone recognizing any gain. However, this postponement is temporary and the gain reduces the basis of your new home.

Before you can determine the gain from selling your old home, you must know the selling price and the amount realized. The *selling price* is the total you received for the home, including any mortgages or notes assumed by the buyer. The *amount realized* is the selling price less the usual selling expenses per the closing statement.

The gain on sale is the amount realized less the adjusted basis of your home at the time of the sale. (For an explanation of adjusted basis, see page 14.) This gain can be postponed if the purchase price of your new home is *at least as much* as the adjusted sales price of your old home. (If there was business or rental use, make an allocation and compare only the nonbusiness or rental portion of each amount.)

The *adjusted sales price* of your old home is the amount realized less any fixing-up expenses. Fixing-up expenses must not be used when computing the amount realized, are not deductible in determining your taxable income, are not capital improvements, must be paid within 30 days after the sale, and must be for work completed during the 90 days before you sign the contract to sell.

Note that fixing-up expenses can't be deducted in computing the actual gain on the sale of the old home. They are *only* used in figuring the gain on which tax is postponed. To determine the amount of gain that can be postponed, subtract the adjusted sales price of the old home from the cost of the new one. If you reinvest *less* than the adjusted sales price of your old home or simply don't replace it, you may be taxed on some or all of the gain.

Here's an example. Your former home had a basis of $67,500; on February 11, you sold it for $92,100, with selling expenses amounting to $7,500. During the 90-day period ending February 11, you had the entire house painted for $1,200 and made improvements totaling $1,100. These were paid for on March 5 (within 30 days after the sale). Within the required time you purchased and moved into a new home that cost $81,900. Here's how to compute the amount of gain on which tax is not postponed, the amount that is postponed, and the basis of your new home:

1.	Selling price of old home	$92,100	
2.	Less selling expenses	(7,500)	
3.	Amount realized		$84,600
4.	Basis of old home	$67,500	
5.	Add cost of improvements	1,100	
6.	Adjusted basis of old home		(68,600)
7.	Gain on old home (line 3 less line 6)		$16,000
8.	Amount realized on old home, line 3 above	$84,600	
9.	Less fixing-up expenses	(1,200)	
10.	Adjusted sales price of old home		$83,400
11.	Cost of new home		(81,900)
12.	Taxable gain (line 10 less line 11)		$ 1,500
13.	Postponed gain (line 7 less line 12)		$14,500
14.	Cost of new home		$81,900
15.	Less gain postponed (line 13)		(14,500)
16.	Basis of new home		$67,400

Business or rental use of your home. You cannot postpone recognizing gain on the business portion when you've deducted expenses for the business or rental use of your home in the year of sale. In this case, you must allocate the gain (or loss) between the business (or rental) portion and the personal portion, dividing the selling price, selling expenses, and property's basis between the two. Base the allocation on the percentage of business use. You're required to reduce the basis of the business portion by any depreciation.

If you've permanently converted your former home to rental property and you subsequently sell it, the basis used will depend on whether there's a gain or loss on the sale. If there's a gain, simply use the adjusted basis on the date of the sale. If there's a loss, you must use the lesser of the adjusted basis or fair market value at the time it was converted. (If the latter is used, you're allowed to increase this amount by the cost of improvements and reduce it for depreciation claimed since the conversion date.)

The gain (or loss) on the business or rental portion is reported on Form 4797. Under the Tax Reform Act of 1986, such a gain (or loss) is either taxed or deductible at capital gains rates, as ordinary income (because of depreciation recapture), or a combination of the two. Note that in 1987, the maximum capital gains rate increases from 20% to 28%. Beginning in 1988, the tax rate on capital gains will be the same as on any other income.

If you had a home office but didn't meet all the strict rules for deducting home office expenses in the year of sale, all the gain, business and non-business, can be postponed, assuming the purchase of your new home meets all the other requirements for this treatment.

Tax$aver Tip. *The easiest way to avoid recognizing any gain is to make sure that you don't meet the home office rules in the year of sale.*

Exclusion of gain at age 55. If you or your spouse has reached the age of 55 by the date your principal home is sold, you may exclude up to $125,000 of the gain from gross income ($62,500 if spouses file separate returns). You must have owned and occupied the home as your principal residence for at least 3 out of the 5 years prior to the date of sale or exchange and neither spouse can ever have excluded gain on any home sold after July 26, 1978. This exclusion of gain must be elected and is available on only *one* sale in your lifetime.

You're not required to reinvest in another home when you elect this exclusion, but you can couple it with the postponement of gain provisions if you wish to purchase another residence that's more expensive.

Trading homes. When you trade homes (usually through a real estate dealer), it's treated as if a sale and a purchase occurred. Any trade-in allowance is considered as the sales price, whether or not the real estate dealer assumed your mortgage. As long as the selling price (before the trade-in allowance) of the new home is more than the sales price of the old one, you must postpone the gain. The basis will be the new home's selling price less the postponed gain.

Nontaxable, like-kind exchanges. No gain or loss is recognized for tax purposes, even if realized on the exchange, if the business portion of the replacement property is basically the same as what you had before the exchange. Several conditions must be met:

1. The property held and received by you must be business or rental property and must qualify under the rules.
2. It must be an exchange of like property.
3. Within 45 days after the trade date, the property you are to receive must be specifically identified.
4. You must receive the property before the earlier of the 181st day after the trade date, or the date (including extensions) your tax return is due for the year of the trade date.

If the trade is partially for cash or property not considered as like-kind but all other conditions are met, you'll be taxed only on the portion of the gain not considered as like-kind. A similar proportionate part of a loss is not deductible.

The basis of property received in such an exchange is usually the adjusted basis of the traded property. Increase this amount by cash paid, additional costs, and any recognized gain. Reduce it by cash or unlike property received and any recognized loss.

Installment sales. When you sell your home and all or a portion of the selling price is paid directly to you over a period of time by the buyer, you probably have an installment sale. If you had a gain on the sale, the law allows you to report only a proportionate amount of profit each year based on payments actually received.

Suppose you sold your home for $100,000 and had a $20,000 gain on the sale, a gross profit of 20%. You grant a second mortgage to the buyer for $10,000 to be paid back to you over 10 years. If you were paid $1,000 each year, you would report 20%, or $200, as income each year.

Starting with the year of sale, you must report income from an installment sale on Form 6252. This method of reporting income applies automatically to qualified sales unless you elect *not* to have it apply. Such an election must be made on or before the date your tax return is due for the year of sale. Under the Tax Reform Act of 1986, the use of the installment method is limited for certain sales of business or rental property when the selling price exceeds $150,000. See your tax advisor if this applies to you.

Proration of real estate taxes. When you sell your home, your real estate tax deduction must be prorated between you and the buyer according to the number of days each owned the property. Your closing statement should show that you're allocated for days up to, but not including, the date of sale. There's a tax break for sellers when due to local law, the buyer is personally liable for paying the tax. The seller is considered to have paid the amount imposed on the date of sale and can deduct it, even though it's later paid by the buyer.

Sometimes, due to local law, you've already paid the entire tax bill on property you later decide to sell. In this case, your allocated share of taxes represents income if you deducted the full amount in an earlier year, since part of it has now been repaid to you. Depending on the amounts, you'll need to figure what portion, if any, should be included in income. If the allocation and the added income occur in the same tax year, simply deduct the net amount as real estate taxes. ■

The federal or state government, or a political subdivision with the proper authority, can legally condemn or threaten to condemn your private property for public use. In return, you may either receive other property, which may or may not be similar, or receive cash in the form of insurance proceeds or a condemnation award. This kind of compulsory action is called an involuntary conversion or exchange. Depending on your property's adjusted basis at the time, you may have a loss or a gain from the exchange or sale.

The following discussion is a cursory look at the situations you might encounter when property you own is condemned. Since condemnation rules are complex and the amounts involved are usually significant, consult an attorney and your tax advisor at the earliest possible date.

Types of awards. *Condemnation awards* can be money, the value of property you receive for your condemned property, or the proceeds from a sale due to a threatened or imminent condemnation. Included as part of the award are any amounts withheld by the condemning authority to pay debts on your property. Excluded is any interest paid due to delays in payment of your award—it's simply reported separately as ordinary income. A net condemnation award is the total award less expenses (such as legal, engineering, and appraisal fees) you paid to secure it.

Severance damages is compensation paid to you because the portion of the condemned property you're allowed to retain declines in value. The agreed-upon amount should be put in writing; otherwise, it will be considered as a condemnation award.

To determine net severance damages, first subtract the expenses of securing them (allocated between condemnation and severance awards); then reduce them by any special assessment levied against your retained property and withheld from your condemnation award. This net amount reduces the basis of your retained property. If net severance damages are greater than the basis, you have a gain, which may then be postponed either by buying replacement property or by restoring the retained property to its former use.

Consequential damage awards result when your property is not actually taken by the governmental authority but suffers damages from public improvements made by that authority. Consequential awards are treated the same as severance damages.

Special assessments must be actually withheld in order to be subtracted from award proceeds. These assessments are usually levied when the property you retained is benefited by the improvement resulting from the condemnation. They are first subtracted from severance damages, with any remaining balance subtracted from the condemnation award.

Computing gain or loss. You compute gain or loss by comparing the adjusted basis (see page 14) of your condemned property with the award received (less expenses of securing it). If the result is a loss, it's deductible in the tax year it occurred only if

it's business or investment property. (A condemnation loss on a personal residence is not deductible.) If the result is a gain, you can defer paying tax on it if you purchase qualified replacement property within 2 years for nonbusiness property or 3 years for real property used in a trade or business or for investment purposes. Qualified replacement property must be used similarly to that of the condemned property.

If you received property, not cash, from the condemning authority, there's also no gain recognized if the acquired property is similar or related in service or use to the property condemned.

When a residence that's condemned is used partly for rental or business, each portion must be treated as a separate piece of property and gain or loss must be computed for each part.

For an example of how to determine your gain or loss, suppose you have a duplex, live in one unit, and rent out the other one. You then sell it for $36,000 under a threat of condemnation. Originally, you paid $38,000 for the duplex and spent $2,000 for a new roof. You claimed allowable depreciation of $6,900 for the rental part of the property and spent $400 in legal fees in connection with the sale. Your gain or loss is figured as follows:

	Residential Unit	Rental Unit
Amount of award received	$18,000	$18,000
Less legal expenses	(200)	(200)
Net condemnation award (A)	$17,800	$17,800
Adjusted basis of each unit		
½ of original cost	$19,000	$19,000
½ of cost of roof	1,000	1,000
Depreciation on rental unit		(6,900)
Adjusted basis of each (B)	$20,000	$13,100
Nondeductible loss on residential unit (A) – (B)	($ 2,200)	
Gain on rental unit (A) – (B)		$ 4,700 ∎

Deducting Moving Expenses

Employees and people who are self-employed can deduct job-related moving expenses, regardless of whether they're just entering the work force, they were transferred, or they quit and found a new job on their own, as long as they satisfy certain tests. Self-employed people must move for legitimate business reasons to qualify for the deduction.

Under the provisions of the Tax Reform Act of 1986, these deductions are now available *only* as itemized deductions, even for the self-employed. The tests you must meet and the limitations that apply to such deductions are discussed below.

Record your moving expenses in the register on page 129. Use the log on page 130 for travel, meals, and lodging expenses.

Tests You Must Meet

In order to be deductible, your move must be closely related in time and place to beginning work in the new location. The expenses must be incurred within a year from the time you first start working at the new job or business, unless you can prove that extenuating circumstances prevented you from moving sooner. Also, it's usually not considered closely related in place to starting work if the distance from your new home to the new job site is greater than the distance from your old home to the new job location. Despite this rule, a move may be considered closely related in place to the start of work if living in your new home is a condition of employment or if you'll spend *less* time or money commuting because of the move. The homes at both locations must be your principal residence, not a vacation home you own.

Time test. Employees must work full-time for at least 39 weeks during the first 12 months after arriving at the new job location to meet this test. Self-employed people must satisfy this same test and also work full-time for at least 78 weeks during the first 24 months after arrival. Full time is what's considered customary for your type of work, you can work for more than one employer, and you don't have to work 39 weeks in a row. (Failure to meet the time test is discussed later.)

For married couples who both work, only one has to satisfy the full-time work test if they file jointly. Otherwise, each must meet the test and deduct only their *own* expenses.

The time test doesn't have to be met if you're disabled, you're laid off or fired (but not for willful misconduct), or you transfer for your employer's benefit.

Distance test. This test can best be understood if you complete the following:

1. Enter the number of miles from your *former* home to your *new* principal work place: _____

2. Enter the number of miles from your *former* home to your *former* principal work place: (   )

3. Subtract line 2 from line 1:   _____

If line 3 is 35 miles or more, you've satisfied this test. If it's less, you can't claim *any* moving expense deductions. If you had no former

principal place of work, your new job site must be at least 35 miles from your former residence.

Use the shortest route between the locations to figure the distances. Your principal place of work is where you'll spend the most time, where your work is centered, or where you'll work permanently (not temporarily). When you work for more than one employer, your principal work place will depend on time spent, amount of work done, and income earned at each location.

Deductible Expenses

Numerous expenses connected with moving are deductible. They must be reasonable considering the circumstances of your move.

Moving household goods and personal items. Whether you move yourself or hire someone to move you, the cost of packing and moving household belongings from your old home to your new one is deductible. Household members must have lived in the former home *and* in the new one. Included are the costs of shipping your car, storage, and insurance within any consecutive 30-day period from the time your goods are moved out to the time they're delivered.

Travel between old and new residences. The costs of travel, meals, and lodging while en route to your new home are deductible for your entire household, beginning on the day before you actually leave and ending on the day you arrive. Only *one* trip is deductible.

Pre-move house-hunting expenses. If you make house-hunting trips, you can deduct—up to certain limits—the costs of travel, meals, and lodging while you're traveling to and from the new area and also while you're there. However, to be deductible, such trips must take place *after* you've obtained a job in the new area.

If you're self-employed, you must have made "substantial" arrangements (determined by the IRS on a case-by-case basis) to begin work at the new location. Your attempts to find a new residence need not be successful for the expense to be deductible, and there's no limit on the number of trips you or the members of your household may make.

Temporary living expenses. You can deduct *meal* and *lodging* expenses (up to certain limits) for a 30-day period after you move *if* you're in temporary quarters. However, rent you pay for a home you plan to purchase and any other personal living expenses for you or members of your family are *not* deductible.

Expenses of disposing of your old home. Deductible as moving expenses are costs (limited in amount) connected with the sale or disposition of your former home, such as escrow, legal and title fees, loan placement charges, points, real estate commissions, state transfer taxes, and the like. Some of these expenses may be taken as an itemized deduction instead. Or you can treat them as selling expenses, which would reduce any gain you had on the sale. (You'll have to decide how to treat each one in view of the limitations and other tax-planning considerations.)

Renters who must end an unexpired lease can deduct all payments related to the early release. Also deductible is the difference between rent you must continue to pay and any rent you receive from subleasing your former home.

Expenses of buying your new home. If you buy a new home, certain acquisition costs, such as appraisals, escrow, and legal and title fees, are deductible as moving expenses (subject to limitations). Or these expenses can be added to basis. Again, do what works best for you in view of the limitations discussed below. If you lease your new home, you can't deduct any rental payments or security deposits. You can, however, deduct commissions and legal fees associated with acquiring the lease.

Travel by car. To compute moving-related auto expenses, the IRS allows you to use either the standard 9¢ per mile rate, plus parking and tolls, or deduct your actual costs of gas, oil, parking, tolls, and repairs (occurring on the trip). The actual cost method usually results in the larger deduction, but figure it both ways to be sure. No deductions are allowed for depreciation, insurance, or repairs resulting from an accident.

Claiming Your Expenses

Claim moving expenses on Form 3903, either in the year you incurred the expenses or in the year you paid them. However, if you receive any reimbursements or allowances in kind (such as using the company credit card) for your move, it's best to claim the deductions in the same year you receive the reimbursement. Reimbursements should be reported as income in the year received, and you should be supplied a W-2 form.

Failing to meet the time test. If you deduct the expenses and later on don't meet the time test, you can either amend the prior return, eliminating that deduction and paying additional tax, or simply include the total amount of your previously claimed moving expense deduction in other income in the year you fail to meet the test.

Limitations on deductions. Though there are no limits on the deductibility of amounts spent for moving household goods and traveling to your new home, the combined total of all *other* moving expenses for married people filing jointly, for one working spouse, or for single people can't exceed $3,000, of which no more than $1,500 can be for house-hunting trips and temporary living expenses combined. (If you're married and filing separately, the limitations are half the above amounts.)

Because of these limitations, you need to be very careful about how you classify your expenditures. It's best to consult your tax advisor in order to maximize your deductions.

Different rules apply for members of the armed forces, retired people or survivors, and people on temporary assignments, to name a few. For more information, ask the IRS for Publication 521: *Moving Expenses.* ■

Logs & Registers

Record Keeping Made Easy

The various logs and registers you'll need to keep track of your deductible expenses throughout the year, as well as forms to help you compute your allowable deductions, are explained on the following pages.

Adjusted Basis of Home Since Acquisition (page 84). Begin by figuring your original basis on the date you bought your home; then summarize all increases and decreases to basis since that date up to December 31 of last year. Record all changes in the current year and transfer the basis at year-end to next year's book.

Log of Home Improvements (page 85). Use this log to record improvements and additions either in the current year or prior years; at the end of the year, transfer the totals to the form above.

Deductible Expense Register (page 86). Use this register to record, categorize, and total all your deductible expenses, regardless of the method of payment. Be sure to stay up to date by making entries on a regular basis. Transfer your monthly totals to the annual summary on pages 110–111.

The register allows you to separate the expenses that *must* be allocated based on the percentage of your home used for business or rental purposes. (How to allocate your expenses and compute your total deduction is explained on pages 78–80.)

For each payment by check, simply list the requested information. If you have large and frequent business expenses, you may want to maintain a separate checking account for them.

For payments by credit card, either enter each expense as incurred or wait until you receive your monthly statement, write one check, and distribute the expenses to the proper columns.

For payments made in cash, be sure to get and retain receipts, and record the expenditures as soon as possible.

Tax$aver Tips. *Pay all bills for deductible expenses before year-end so they'll be deductible that year. Note that the law allows you to deduct credit card charges in the year incurred, even if payment occurs the following year.*

Don't claim large amounts on your return for categories such as miscellaneous or other expenses. Instead, identify large amounts separately and show other expenses as smaller amounts.

Daily Log of Home Office or Computer Equipment Use (page 112).

This log will help you record, compute, and document the following required information:

- Total hours the part of your home was used for trade or business purposes
- Total hours a home computer was used for all purposes, as well as for trade or business
- Percentage of business use of a home computer

This form will document that you used the business space on a regular basis. Provide as much detail as possible right on the log—what was accomplished, whom you met with, and so on.

When you have a home computer, you're faced with allocating the time it's *actually* used (rather than merely being available for use) between business and personal use. On the log, record the number of hours the equipment was used for business and investment purposes and the total number of hours it was used for *any* purpose during the year. If you keep a running total by page, you'll have an idea of how your percentage is developing during the year so you can limit personal use if necessary and ensure that you'll meet the 50% test. Keep a record of dates and hours your computer is used at all locations.

Transfer the totals from this log to the form on page 119 to compute your percentages.

Computation of Business Use Percentages (BUP) (page 117).

Before you can compute your final deduction, you must determine the percentage of business use of your home. The IRS allows you to do this by any reasonable method. Generally, however, only two are used (the form has space for figuring percentages both ways).

For the *room-by-room method,* you divide the number of rooms, or fractions thereof, used for business by the total number of rooms in your home. (Use this method only if the rooms are comparable in size; don't count a utility room or bathrooms.)

For the *square-footage method,* you need to know the square footage both of the space used for business and of the entire home. Include all areas, but exclude an attached garage if it's only used to park cars. Be sure to include *all* space used for business, even if it's a portion of a room, such as a closet. Garage storage and shelving used for business should also be measured.

Once you've figured the total space used for business, divide it by the total square feet of your home to arrive at your BUP.

Tax$aver Tip. *If you think that all your rooms are about the same size, compute your BUP both ways and use the larger figure for computing your deductions.*

Computation of Business Use Expenses (page 117).
Expenses of operating your home fall into one of three categories: business or direct expenses deductible in full, indirect expenses that are partially deductible, or expenses completely unrelated to business and not deductible at all. Transfer the annual totals from the Deductible Expense Register to this form and make the indicated computations to arrive at your total deductions *before* considering the limitations.

Expenses deductible in full are called *direct* expenses, since they benefit *only* the part of your home used for business. Decorating and making repairs to the room used are good examples. Direct expenses of a day-care facility must be further allocated (see page 42). Though fully deductible, all direct expenses are still subject to the deduction limitation discussed later.

Partially deductible expenses are referred to as *indirect* expenses, since they benefit the entire home, not just the personal or business portion. Only the *business* portion is deductible (you apply your BUP against the amounts paid). Examples of indirect expenses include real estate taxes and interest on any mortgage, and repairs that benefit the *entire* home.

Nondeductible expenses are those that benefit only the *nonbusiness* portion of your home, such as landscaping, gardening and lawn care, and repairs to personal areas of your home. You also can't deduct an amount equal to the fair rental value of the business part of your home.

Once you've determined the expenses deductible in full and those subject to allocation, you're ready to consider the effect of the limitations on your deduction.

Computation of Deduction Limitations (page 118). The primary purpose of the limitation is to prevent expenses resulting from the business use of your home from *creating* or *increasing* a net loss from such activities. The form is designed to help you determine which of the limitation levels apply to you. Depending on the amount of your *net*, not gross, income (effective in 1987), you may be able to deduct all, some, or none of your direct and indirect expenses.

To determine gross income, the starting point in applying the limitations, you may only include income from qualifying business use derived from the business use of your home. When the gross income from your trade or business is derived from more than one location, you have to make an allocation on some reasonable basis. (Use the log on page 112 to help you document your time.)

To determine net income, as now required by the Tax Reform Act of 1986, subtract from gross income all trade or business expenses not subject to allocation or limitation. Transfer this amount to the form and subtract your remaining expenses in this order: the business portion of mortgage interest, real estate taxes, and casualty losses; direct and indirect expenses other than depreciation; and last, depreciation expense.

Beginning in 1987, the new law allows home office deductions disallowed solely because of the income limitations to be carried forward to later years. And remember that any portion of mortgage interest, real estate taxes, and casualty losses *not* claimed as a home office deduction can generally be deducted on Schedule A if you itemize.

Keep in mind that even if the rules restrict or eliminate your deductions for direct and indirect expenses, you can still deduct business expenses that don't relate to the business use of your home.

Tax$aver Tip. *Claiming deductions for the business use of your home is a controversial audit issue with the IRS. Reduce your chances of being audited by attaching copies of the forms for computing BUP, business use expenses, and deduction limitations directly to your tax return.*

Record of Vacation Home Use & Rent Collected (page 120).

Use this form to keep track of all uses during the year. At the end of the year, you'll know if the limitation rules apply and the amount of total rents collected (see page 45).

Computation of Rental Deduction Limitations (page 123).

Here you can compute your deduction limitation, using the method that's most advantageous to you (see page 47).

Deductible Entertainment Expense Record (page 124).

With this form, you can satisfy the strict record-keeping requirements for business entertainment. Be sure to note which test was met and when the entertainment and business discussion took place.

Moving Expense Register (page 129).

Use this form to categorize your moving expenses. Classify your expenses carefully, since some expenses are limited (see page 73).

Log of Deductible Travel for Moving Purposes (page 130).

Record all travel and meal expenses here, again being sure to describe the reason for each trip. If you travel by car, keep receipts for gas and oil; then compare your actual expenses with the amount allowable at the 9¢-per-mile rate.

Deduction Checklist

Here are some deductions (taken either in the year of purchase or through depreciation) you may overlook. Those mentioned in the text are not repeated here. For more information, see *Sunset's Home Office Tax$aver* and *Itemized Deductions Tax$aver*.

Interest Payments

Below-market interest rate loans
Condominium owner's and cooperative housing
    tenant-shareholder's proportionate share of
    points and interest
Cosigner's interest paid if jointly liable for a debt
Interest paid on unimproved real property
Late payment charges if not for specific services

Real Estate Taxes

Condominium owner's proportionate share of
    taxes on own unit and common areas of
    building and grounds
Essential or special services only if imposed at a
    uniform rate on users and all owners of
    designated properties
Tax paid by shareholders in a cooperative
    housing corporation (pro rata share only)
Tax paid on a residence owned solely by one
    spouse where ex-spouse occupied it rent-free

Home Office Direct Expenses

Air conditioner (portable)
Carpets, drapes
Items with a useful life of less than a year

Home Office Indirect Expenses

Central air conditioning system
Depreciation
Insurance premiums on home
Utilities, sewer, water, trash collection

Trade or Business Expenses

Books, technical references, professional or
    trade journals, subscriptions
Conventions and trade shows
Furniture and equipment rental
Gifts (under $25 per person)
Pictures, lamps, mirrors, clocks
Small tools and supplies
Casual labor
Tax$aver series
Telephone answering machine

Rental Expenses

Advertising
Auto and travel
Cleaning and supplies
Legal fees
Professional fees
Repairs and maintenance

81

Claiming Deductions on Your Return

Where you claim your deductible expenses depends on your income-earning status. *Employees* who incur no reimbursed or unreimbursed expenses will simply either have enough deductions to itemize or will use the standard deduction. Those with such expenses will continue to use Form 2106, with the excess of expenses over reimbursements (or unreimbursed expenses) being deducted as a miscellaneous deduction on Schedule A. Such deductions are now subject to a limitation of 2% of adjusted gross income.

Sole owners of a business should use Schedule C to report their trade or business expenses, including any home office deductions. However, the new tax law says that moving expenses for *all* taxpayers must be reported on Schedule A.

Investors in securities claim their expenses on Schedule A as miscellaneous deductions, now subject to the 2% of adjusted gross income limitation. Investors in real estate use Schedule E. ∎

Tax$aver Tip. *Many taxpayers assume early in the year that they won't have enough deductions to itemize. Unless you're aware of what's available and keep track of your deductible expenses on a regular basis, you could be making an assumption that's costing you money. If you write down your expenses throughout the year, you'll at least give yourself an option at year-end.*

Record of Important Information & Dates

Personal Information

Name_____ Address _____

City _____ State _____ Zip _____

Telephone: Home _____ Business _____

Tax Advisor

Name_____ Address _____

City _____ State _____ Zip _____

Telephone: Business _____ Home _____

Automobile Information

Odometer Reading Jan. 1, 19____: _____ Dec. 31, 19____: _____

Year & Make _____ Model _____ Colors _____

Vehicle ID No. _____ Weight _____ Lbs.

State License Plate No. _____ Expiration Date _____

State Driver's License No. _____ Expiration Date _____

Credit Card Information

Card Issued by	Account Number	Expiration Date

Insurance Information

Company _____ Telephone _____

Agent _____ Telephone _____

Policy for_____ Limits _____

Annual Premium _____ Term _____ to _____

Policy for_____ Limits _____

Annual Premium _____ Term _____ to _____

Policy for _____ Limits _____

Annual Premium _____ Term _____ to _____

Loss Payable Clause to _____

Business Use Percentages

Year	Home Office	Automobile	Home Computer
Current 19__			
Prior 19__			
2nd Prior 19__			

Important I.D. Numbers & Dates

Description	Number	Expiration Date or Payment Due
Federal Business ID #		
State Business ID #		
State & Local Business Licenses		
State & Local Property Taxes		

Adjusted Basis of Home Since Acquisition

Original Basis, Date Acquired _____ 19 ___	$		**Subtotal (from below)**	$	
Plus All Increases to Basis to Dec. 31 of Last Year			Other Increases to Basis _____		
Less All Decreases to Basis to Dec. 31 of Last Year	(	)	_____		
Adjusted Basis at Beginning of Current Year	$		_____		
Increases to Basis during Year					
Improvements to Property _____			**Subtotal**	$	
			Decreases to Basis during Year		
_____			Postponed Gain on Former Home		
_____			Depreciation Due to Business Use		
_____			Depreciation Due to Rental Use		
Additions to Property _____			Casualty Loss Reimbursed		
_____			Casualty Loss Deducted (Not Reimbursed)		
_____			Other Decreases to Basis _____		
_____			_____		
Interest & Taxes during Construction Not Claimed as Deductions					
Closing Costs Due to Refinancing			**Total Decreases**	(	)
Subtotal	$		**Adjusted Basis, Year Ended _____ 19 ___**	$	

og of Home Improvements

Date 19___	Paid to	Description of Work Done	Payment		Function			Total Cost	
			Check Number	Cr. Card or Loan	Ext. Life	Incr. Value	More Useful		

Deductible Expense Register for Month of _____ 19 ___

Date 19___	Paid to/Description	Check #, Cash, or Cr. Card	Itemized Deductions on Schedule A								Direct Business or Rental Expenses Subject to Limitation	
			Home Mortgage Interest	Real Estate Taxes							Description	Amount
1/6	C & S Office Products	Cash										
1/14	Paul's Carpets	128									Carpet cleaning	35 00
Note: See page 76 for instructions.		Subtotals										

Business or Rental Expenses Subject to Allocation & Limitation						Business or Rental Expenses Not Subject to Allocation								
Home Mortgage Interest	Real Estate Taxes	Utilities & Other Services	Insurance on Home	Repairs & Maint.		Car & Truck	Travel	Phone	Office & Operating Supplies			**Other Expenses**		
												Description	Amount	
									22 45			ans. machine	98	77

Deductible Expense Register for Month of _____ 19 ___

Date 19___	Paid to/Description	Check #, Cash, or Cr. Card	Itemized Deductions on Schedule A							Direct Business or Rental Expenses Subject to Limitation	
			Home Mortgage Interest	Real Estate Taxes						Description	Amount
Note: See page 76 for instructions.		Subtotals									

88

Business or Rental Expenses Subject to Allocation & Limitation						Business or Rental Expenses Not Subject to Allocation							
Home Mortgage Interest	Real Estate Taxes	Utilities & Other Services	Insurance on Home	Repairs & Maint.		Car & Truck	Travel	Phone	Office & Operating Supplies			Other Expenses	
												Description	Amount

Deductible Expense Register for Month of _____ 19 ___

Date 19___	Paid to/Description	Check #, Cash, or Cr. Card	Itemized Deductions on Schedule A								Direct Business or Rental Expenses Subject to Limitation	
			Home Mortgage Interest	Real Estate Taxes							Description	Amount
	Note: See page 76 for instructions.	Subtotals										

Business or Rental Expenses Subject to Allocation & Limitation						Business or Rental Expenses Not Subject to Allocation							
Home Mortgage Interest	Real Estate Taxes	Utilities & Other Services	Insurance on Home	Repairs & Maint.		Car & Truck	Travel	Phone	Office & Operating Supplies			Other Expenses	
												Description	Amount

Deductible Expense Register for Month of _____ 19 ___

Date 19___	Paid to/Description	Check #, Cash, or Cr. Card	Itemized Deductions on Schedule A								Direct Business or Rental Expenses Subject to Limitation	
			Home Mortgage Interest	Real Estate Taxes							Description	Amount
Note: See page 76 for instructions.		**Subtotals**										

92

Business or Rental Expenses Subject to Allocation & Limitation						Business or Rental Expenses Not Subject to Allocation							
Home Mortgage Interest	Real Estate Taxes	Utilities & Other Services	Insurance on Home	Repairs & Maint.		Car & Truck	Travel	Phone	Office & Operating Supplies			Other Expenses	
												Description	Amount

Deductible Expense Register for Month of _____ 19 ___

Date 19___	Paid to/Description	Check #, Cash, or Cr. Card	Itemized Deductions on Schedule A							Direct Business or Rental Expenses Subject to Limitation	
			Home Mortgage Interest	Real Estate Taxes						Description	Amount
Note: See page 76 for instructions.		Subtotals									

94

Business or Rental Expenses Subject to Allocation & Limitation						Business or Rental Expenses Not Subject to Allocation							
Home Mortgage Interest	Real Estate Taxes	Utilities & Other Services	Insurance on Home	Repairs & Maint.		Car & Truck	Travel	Phone	Office & Operating Supplies			Other Expenses	
												Description	Amount

Deductible Expense Register for Month of _____ 19 ___

Date 19___	Paid to/Description	Check #, Cash, or Cr. Card	Itemized Deductions on Schedule A							Direct Business or Rental Expenses Subject to Limitation	
			Home Mortgage Interest	Real Estate Taxes						Description	Amount
Note: See page 76 for instructions.		Subtotals									

Business or Rental Expenses Subject to Allocation & Limitation						Business or Rental Expenses Not Subject to Allocation							
Home Mortgage Interest	Real Estate Taxes	Utilities & Other Services	Insurance on Home	Repairs & Maint.		Car & Truck	Travel	Phone	Office & Operating Supplies			Other Expenses	
												Description	Amount

Deductible Expense Register for Month of _____ 19 ____

Date 19__	Paid to/Description	Check #, Cash, or Cr. Card	Itemized Deductions on Schedule A							Direct Business or Rental Expenses Subject to Limitation	
			Home Mortgage Interest	Real Estate Taxes						Description	Amount
Note: See page 76 for instructions.		**Subtotals**									

98

Business or Rental Expenses Subject to Allocation & Limitation						Business or Rental Expenses Not Subject to Allocation						Other Expenses	
Home Mortgage Interest	Real Estate Taxes	Utilities & Other Services	Insurance on Home	Repairs & Maint.		Car & Truck	Travel	Phone	Office & Operating Supplies			Description	Amount

Deductible Expense Register for Month of _____ 19 ___

Date 19___	Paid to/Description	Check #, Cash, or Cr. Card	Itemized Deductions on Schedule A							Direct Business or Rental Expenses Subject to Limitation	
			Home Mortgage Interest	Real Estate Taxes						Description	Amount
Note: See page 76 for instructions.	Subtotals										

100

Business or Rental Expenses Subject to Allocation & Limitation						Business or Rental Expenses Not Subject to Allocation							
Home Mortgage Interest	Real Estate Taxes	Utilities & Other Services	Insurance on Home	Repairs & Maint.		Car & Truck	Travel	Phone	Office & Operating Supplies			Other Expenses	
												Description	Amount

Deductible Expense Register for Month of _____ 19 ___

Date 19___	Paid to/Description	Check #, Cash, or Cr. Card	Itemized Deductions on Schedule A							Direct Business or Rental Expenses Subject to Limitation	
			Home Mortgage Interest	Real Estate Taxes						Description	Amount
Note: See page 76 for instructions.		**Subtotals**									

102

Business or Rental Expenses Subject to Allocation & Limitation						Business or Rental Expenses Not Subject to Allocation							
Home Mortgage Interest	Real Estate Taxes	Utilities & Other Services	Insurance on Home	Repairs & Maint.		Car & Truck	Travel	Phone	Office & Operating Supplies			Other Expenses	
												Description	Amount

Deductible Expense Register for Month of _____ 19 ___

Date 19___	Paid to/Description	Check #, Cash, or Cr. Card	Itemized Deductions on Schedule A							Direct Business or Rental Expenses Subject to Limitation	
			Home Mortgage Interest	Real Estate Taxes						Description	Amount
Note: See page 76 for instructions.		**Subtotals**									

| Business or Rental Expenses Subject to Allocation & Limitation ||||||| Business or Rental Expenses Not Subject to Allocation ||||||||||
| Home Mortgage Interest || Real Estate Taxes || Utilities & Other Services || Insurance on Home || Repairs & Maint. ||| Car & Truck || Travel || Phone || Office & Operating Supplies |||||| Other Expenses ||
																					Description	Amount

Deductible Expense Register for Month of _____ 19 ____

Date 19__	Paid to/Description	Check #, Cash, or Cr. Card	Itemized Deductions on Schedule A							Direct Business or Rental Expenses Subject to Limitation	
			Home Mortgage Interest	Real Estate Taxes						Description	Amount
Note: See page 76 for instructions.		Subtotals									

Business or Rental Expenses Subject to Allocation & Limitation						Business or Rental Expenses Not Subject to Allocation							
Home Mortgage Interest	Real Estate Taxes	Utilities & Other Services	Insurance on Home	Repairs & Maint.		Car & Truck	Travel	Phone	Office & Operating Supplies			Other Expenses	
												Description	Amount

Deductible Expense Register for Month of _____ 19 ___

Date 19___	Paid to/Description	Check #, Cash, or Cr. Card	Itemized Deductions on Schedule A							Direct Business or Rental Expenses Subject to Limitation	
			Home Mortgage Interest	Real Estate Taxes						Description	Amount
Note: See page 76 for instructions.		Subtotals									

Business or Rental Expenses Subject to Allocation & Limitation						Business or Rental Expenses Not Subject to Allocation								
Home Mortgage Interest	Real Estate Taxes	Utilities & Other Services	Insurance on Home	Repairs & Maint.		Car & Truck	Travel	Phone	Office & Operating Supplies			Other Expenses		
												Description	Amount	

Annual Summary of Deductible Expense Register for 19 _____

| Month | Itemized Deductions on Schedule A | | | | | | | Direct Business or Rental Expenses Subject to Limitation | | Business or Rental | |
	Home Mortgage Interest	Real Estate Taxes						Description	Amount	Home Mortgage Interest	Real Estate Taxes
January											
February											
March											
April											
May											
June											
July											
August											
September											
October											
November											
December											
Totals for Year											

Expenses Subject to Allocation & Limitation				Business or Rental Expenses Not Subject to Allocation							Other Expenses		Monthly Totals	
Utilities & Other Services	Insurance on Home	Repairs & Maint.		Car & Truck	Travel	Phone	Office & Operating Supplies				Description	Amount		

Daily Log of Home Office or Computer Equipment Use

Date 19 __	Description of Use	Hours of Use			Purpose of Use (Allocated by Time)			
		From	To	Total Hours	Trade or Business	Invest-ment	Personal	
1/6	Meeting with J. Franklin re mailing	1:30 pm	4:45 pm	3 1/4	3 1/4			
Note: See page 77 for instructions.			Subtotals					

Daily Log of Home Office or Computer Equipment Use

Date 19 __	Description of Use	Hours of Use			Purpose of Use (Allocated by Time)			
		From	To	Total Hours	Trade or Business	Invest- ment	Personal	
Note: See page 77 for instructions.		**Subtotals**						

Daily Log of Home Office or Computer Equipment Use

Date 19 __	Description of Use	Hours of Use			Purpose of Use (Allocated by Time)			
		From	To	Total Hours	Trade or Business	Invest-ment	Personal	
Note: See page 77 for instructions.		Subtotals						

Daily Log of Home Office or Computer Equipment Use

Date 19 __	Description of Use	Hours of Use			Purpose of Use (Allocated by Time)			
		From	To	Total Hours	Trade or Business	Invest-ment	Personal	
Note: See page 77 for instructions.		Subtotals						

Daily Log of Home Office or Computer Equipment Use

Date 19 __	Description of Use	Hours of Use			Purpose of Use (Allocated by Time)			
		From	To	Total Hours	Trade or Business	Invest-ment	Personal	
Note: See page 77 for instructions.		**Totals for Year**						

Computation of Business Use Percentages

By Room Basis

Number of Rooms Used for Business .... (A)		
Total Rooms Exclusive of Utility & Bathrooms .... (B)		
Business Use Percentage (A) ÷ (B) .... (C)		%

By Square Footage Basis

Rooms & Areas	Measurements	Total Square Feet	Sq. Ft. Used For Business
	.		
Totals for Entire Home & Business Space			
Business Use Percentage (Bus. Sq. Ft. ÷ Total Sq. Ft.) (D)			%

Business Time Percentage for Day-Care Facilities

Total Hours Facility Was Used during Year	(E)	
Total Hours Available for Use during Year	(F)	
Business Time Percentage (E) ÷ (F)	(G)	%

Computation of Business Use Expenses

Expenses per Annual Summary of Deductible Expense Register

Indirect Expenses Subject to Allocation

Mortgage Interest or Rent	$	
Real Estate Taxes		
Utilities & Other Services		
Insurance for One Year		
Repairs Which Benefit Entire Home		
Depreciation Expense		
Total Indirect Expenses Subject to Allocation	$	
Multiply by BUP (C) or (D)......................	×	%
Total Indirect Expenses (H)	$	

Direct Expenses Deductible in Full

Repairs to Business Part of Home	$	
Painting Business Part of Home		
Other Direct Expenses		
Total Direct Expenses (I)	$	
Total Expenses Subject to Limitation (H) + (I) (J)	$	

For Day-Care Facilities only

Total Indirect Expenses (H) $	×[(C) or (D)]×(G)	(K)	$	
Total Direct Expenses (I) $	× (G)	(L)		
Total Expenses Subject to Limitation (K) + (L)		(M)	$	

117

Computation of Deduction Limitations

Net Income from Business Use of Home (See Note below) . . . . (A) $

Less

  Mortgage Interest ($ X   % BUP) . . . .

  Real Estate Taxes ($ X   % BUP) . . . .

  Casualty Losses ($ X   % BUP) . . . .

    Amount Allowable to Deduct (Total of 3 Prior Lines) . . . . (B)

    Amount Deducted, Lesser of (B) or (A) . . . . (C) $

Limit on Further Deductions (A) Less (C). If Negative, Stop Here. . . . . (D)

Less Direct & Indirect Expenses Other Than Depreciation

  Direct Expenses (Line I or L from Page 117) . . . .

  Indirect Expenses (Line H or K from Page 117, but Reduced by Depreciation Expense Amount) . . . .

    Amount Allowable to Deduct (Total of 2 Prior Lines) . . . . (E)

    Amount Deducted, Lesser of (E) or (D) . . . . (F) $

Limit on Depreciation Deduction (D) Less (F). If Negative, Stop Here. . . . . (G)

Less Depreciation Expense ($ X   % BUP) = Amount Allowable to Deduct . . . . (H)

    Amount Deducted, Lesser of (H) or (G) . . . . (I) $

Note: See page 79 for instructions. Net income is gross income less business expenses unrelated to business use of home, such as supplies and auto expenses. The total of (C), (F), and (I) is the amount you can deduct for the year.

Computation of BUP for Computer Equipment

Computation for Meeting 50% Test	Actual	Example
Total Hours Used for Qualified Trade or Business ....(A)		810
Total Hours Used for All Purposes during Year ....(B)		1,225
BUP for 50% Test (A) ÷ (B) ....(C)	%	66.1%
Computation for Calculating Basis & Depreciation		
Total Hours Used for Investment or Income-Producing Purposes...........................(D)		150
Total Hours Used for Business/Investment (A) + (D) ....(E)		960
BUP for Basis & Depreciation (E) ÷ (B) ....(F)	%	78.4%
Percentage of Personal Use — 100% Less (F)...	%	21.6%

Dates Placed in Service	Date
Computer	
Peripheral Equipment	
_____	
_____	
_____	

Record of Vacation Home Use & Rent Collected

Dates of Use From	To	Rented or Used by / Relationship if Personal	No. of Days Pers.	Rent	Rent Collected Date	Amount		Dates of Use From	To	Rented or Used by / Relationship if Personal	No. of Days Pers.	Rent	Rent Collected Date	Amount	
1/10	1/17	Jeff Evans		7	1/5	500	00								

Record of Vacation Home Use & Rent Collected

Dates of Use		Rented or Used by / Relationship if Personal	No. of Days		Rent Collected		Dates of Use		Rented or Used by / Relationship if Personal	No. of Days		Rent Collected	
From	To		Pers.	Rent	Date	Amount	From	To		Pers.	Rent	Date	Amount

Record of Vacation Home Use & Rent Collected

Dates of Use		Rented or Used by / Relationship if Personal	No. of Days		Rent Collected			Dates of Use		Rented or Used by / Relationship if Personal	No. of Days		Rent Collected	
From	To		Pers.	Rent	Date	Amount		From	To		Pers.	Rent	Date	Amount

Computation of Rental Deduction Limitations

	Rental Personal Method (RPM)		Total Year Method (TYM)	
Total Rental Receipts	$		$	
Less Expenses Paid to Obtain Tenants				
Gross Rental Income as Defined by IRS . . . . (A)				
Less Mortgage Interest ($ × % RPM) ($ × % TYM)				
Real Estate Taxes ($ × % RPM) ($ × % TYM)				
Casualty Losses ($ × % RPM) ($ × % TYM)				
Amount Allowable to Deduct (Total of 3 Prior Lines) . . . . (B)				
Amount Deducted, Lesser of (A) or (B) . . . . (C)				
Limit on Further Deductions, (A) Less (C). If Negative, Stop Here . . . . (D)				
Less Total Operating Expenses ($ × % RPM — Use for TYM Also)				
Total Maintenance Expenses ($ × % RPM — Use for TYM Also)				
Amount Allowable to Deduct (Total of 2 Prior Lines) . . . . (E)				
Amount Deducted, Lesser of (D) or (E) . . . . (F)				
Limit on Depreciation Deduction, (D) Less (F). If Negative, Stop Here . . . . (G)				
Less Depreciation on Dwelling ($ × % RPM — Use for TYM Also)				
Amount Allowable to Deduct . . . . (H)				
Amount Deducted, Lesser of (G) or (H) . . . . (I)				

Note: Be sure to deduct balance of interest (subject to limitations), taxes, and casualty losses on Schedule A if you itemize. See pages 45 and 49 for information on renting and page 47 for an explanation of the two methods.

Deductible Entertainment Expense Record

Date 19___	Names of Those Entertained / Type of Entertainment	Title, Company, or Occupation / Business Relationship	Nature of Discussion & Business Reason or Benefit Received or Expected
1/9	Dan O'Hara / cocktails & dinner	V.P. ATS Co. / supplier	new product introduction

Note: See page 51 for more information on business entertainment.

Length & Location of Business Discussion	Meets Directly Related Test (Yes/No)	Associated with Test Business Discussed during or Directly before or after Meal	Entertainment Costs Food & Beverages				Total		Less Portion for Nonbusiness Guests		Net Entertainment Expenses	
1½ hrs. / den		Directly before	35	50			35	50	(	)	35	50
									(	)		
									(	)		
									(	)		
									(	)		
									(	)		
									(	)		
									(	)		
									(	)		
									(	)		
									(	)		
									(	)		
									(	)		
									(	)		
									(	)		
		Subtotals							(	)		

125

Deductible Entertainment Expense Record

Date 19___	Names of Those Entertained / Type of Entertainment	Title, Company, or Occupation / Business Relationship	Nature of Discussion & Business Reason or Benefit Received or Expected

Note: See page 51 for more information on business entertainment.

Length & Location of Business Discussion	Meets Directly Related Test (Yes/No)	Associated with Test — Business Discussed during or Directly before or after Meal	Entertainment Costs					Total		Less Portion for Nonbusiness Guests		Net Entertainment Expenses	
			Food & Beverages										
										(	)		
										(	)		
										(	)		
										(	)		
										(	)		
										(	)		
										(	)		
										(	)		
										(	)		
										(	)		
										(	)		
										(	)		
										(	)		
										(	)		
										(	)		
										(	)		
		Totals for Year								(	)		

Casualty & Theft Loss Information

Description of Property & Loss Where Located	Date		1 Cost or Other Basis	2 Depr. Allowed or Allowable	3 Salvage Value if Totally Destroyed	4 Adjusted Basis 1−(2+3)	5 Reimb. Received or Expected	6 Gain, if Applic. (5) − (4)	Fair Market Value			Loss (Lesser of 4 or 9, and Less 5)
	Acquired	Loss or Discovery							7 Before Loss	8 After Loss	9 Decrease (7)−(8)	

Note: Transfer information to Form 4684 (Sec. A for personal losses, Sec. B for business losses). Limitations of $100 and 10% of AGI are reflected on Form 4684.

If asset was used for both business and pleasure, allocate loss based on percentage of business use at time of loss or more recent known percentage.

Moving Expense Register

| Date 19___ | Paid to/Description | Ck. #, Cash, or Cr. Card | Moving Household Goods | | Temporary Living Expenses | | Expenses of Old Home | | | | Expenses of New Home | | | |
							Sale/ Exchange		Rent/Lease		Purchase		Lease Acquisition Costs	
Note: See page 80 for instructions.	Totals													

Log of Deductible Travel for Moving Purposes

Date 19 __	Destination & Reason for Trip	Standard Mileage Rate Method					Actual Cost Method	Parking Fees & Tolls		Meals		Lodging				Reimburse-ments	
		Odometer		Computation													
		Start	End	Miles	Rate	Cost	Gas & Oil										
					× 9¢												
					× 9¢												
					× 9¢												
					× 9¢												
					× 9¢												
					× 9¢												
					× 9¢												
					× 9¢												
					× 9¢												
					× 9¢												
					× 9¢												
					× 9¢												
					× 9¢												
					× 9¢												
					× 9¢												
Note: Compute auto expenses using both methods; use the one that gives you the largest deduction (see page 73).		Totals for Year															

Tax Help

Choosing & Working with a Tax Advisor

Many taxpayers hire a tax advisor to prepare their return. Even if you do your own return, you may need the help of a professional tax advisor to solve a particular problem, to prepare for an IRS audit, or to plan for the future. You'll want to choose a qualified advisor you can trust and work with comfortably and confidently.

Who can be a tax advisor? There are more than 20,000 accounting firms in the U.S., and many thousands of people called tax preparers. Only a handful of states require tax preparers to take classes or be licensed.

It's best to retain someone who can legally represent you at all IRS levels. Generally, this person will be a CPA, an attorney, or an "enrolled agent." An enrolled agent must apply to the IRS, pass an examination, and be approved by the IRS to represent taxpayers. Unenrolled tax preparers may represent their clients *only* at the examination level.

Only CPAs, attorneys, and enrolled agents may perform the following on behalf of any taxpayer:

1. Execute claims for a refund.
2. Receive checks in payment of any refund of taxes, penalties, or interest.
3. Execute consents to extend the statutory period for assessment or collection of a tax.
4. Execute closing agreements with respect to a tax liability or specific matter.
5. Delegate authority or substitute another representative.

Fees paid for these services are deductible. Effective in 1987, taxpayers can only deduct them as a miscellaneous deduction, subject to a 2% floor.

Selecting your tax advisor. Many taxpayers don't take the selection process seriously enough. Be cautious and do your homework before you choose. Remember—if your tax preparer makes a mistake or files your return late, it's *you* who will have to pay any additional taxes, penalties, and interest.

Your goals are to find someone who will charge you a fair fee, not do anything that will cause an audit, and be genuinely interested in maximizing your tax savings. Ask friends or business associates whose tax situations might be similar to yours for recommendations, but don't rely on this alone. Do some investigating yourself, check references, and, above all, ask questions.

Before committing yourself, arrange a brief get-acquainted meeting and ask questions such as these:

- What are your areas of tax specialization?
- How do you keep up to date on tax matters?
- What continuing tax education have you undertaken?
- What is your previous tax experience?

Make sure you feel comfortable with the person but be patient—creating a good working relationship can take time.

If you have difficulty finding a competent professional, contact the American Institute of Certified Public Accountants in New York City or the National Society of Public Accountants in Alexandria, Virginia. They can supply you with names of members in good standing in your immediate area.

Some common pitfalls to avoid include retaining anyone who guarantees you a refund or who urges you to claim deductions to which you know you're not entitled, and hiring anyone who bases their fee on the amount of your refund.

Working with a professional. It's important not to just dump your tax records on your tax preparer's desk and have the preparer organize them for you. It will cost you money in increased fees. For best results, follow these guidelines:

- Present all your records in an orderly manner, categorized and summarized (or as requested by the tax preparer).
- Ask about hourly rates and other expenses of people working on your return, and find out how you might help minimize fees.
- Meet the staff people working on your return.
- Ask to receive copies of any correspondence related to you and ask for explanations for each claimed amount you don't understand.
- Before you sign your return, read each line carefully and compare the figures to your own wherever possible. And *never* sign an incomplete return.

- Make sure the tax preparer signs the return that is filed and that you receive a copy.
- If you're being audited, discuss with your tax advisor beforehand how much of each deduction under review may be allowed. Then you'll know when you can be flexible and when you need to stand your ground.
- Before you receive your tax advisor's final bill, ask that any portion of the bill that is not tax-deductible be detailed, to avoid any IRS disallowances.

Other rules and preparers' penalties. According to the IRS code, tax return preparers are subject to criminal penalties if they make an unauthorized disclosure of tax return information or use such information for any purpose other than to prepare a return. There are also penalties for understatement of taxpayer liability. And penalties are assessable for failing to meet the following requirements, unless the failure is due to reasonable cause and not willful neglect:

1. The return must be signed by the person primarily responsible for preparing the return and must also indicate the preparer's and/or firm's identifying number.

2. At the time the return is presented for signing, the taxpayer must be provided with a completed copy of the final return, though this copy need not be signed by the preparer.

3. For 3 years, preparers must keep available for IRS inspection a record of the name, taxpayer ID number, and principal place of work of each tax preparer who worked for them during the period.

4. Effective in 1985, preparers required to sign returns must advise taxpayers of the substantiation requirements of Section 274(d) of the code, related to travel and entertainment expenses, business gifts, and certain depreciation deductions. Preparers should receive assurances that such substantiation exists, but it need not be in writing.

These and other legal requirements have been established by Congress to protect the public against incompetent and dishonest tax preparers. Your awareness of these requirements can help you protect yourself. ∎

Most taxpayers' contact with the IRS is minimal—they file their return and pay their tax or receive a refund, whichever applies. But subsequently, some taxpayers learn that their return has been selected for an audit for any one of a number of reasons. The sections that follow will help you in this and any other dealings with the IRS.

Filing & Amending Your Return

Often, the procedures for filing a return and amending a previously filed return are not well known. Here is some information that may help you.

Filing your return. Always be sure to fill out your return completely, sign it, and file it on time. There are penalties both for late filing and nonpayment, so even if you can't pay then, be sure to send in your return on time.

If you can't make the filing deadline, you can get an automatic 4-month extension by filing Form 4868 and an additional 2-month extension if you have an acceptable reason. You'll be asked to estimate and pay the tax due when filing the extension. If you can't pay the full tax that's due, the IRS will accept an installment payment plan; you'll need to fill out all the necessary papers and agree to a monthly payment plan.

Filing penalties don't apply to a taxpayer entitled to a refund. Also, penalties for late payment can be waived if you have reasonable cause for not paying your tax when due.

Filing an amended return. Whenever you feel the tax you paid, whether resulting from an audit or some other reason, is excessive or incorrect, you have the right to file a claim for a refund. Check first, however, to be sure that no previous form you signed precludes you from filing such a claim. Individual taxpayers should use Form 1040X to file their claims. If you're amending a return for a prior year, you'll need to attach a copy.

You must file an amended return within 3 years of filing the original return or within 2 years from the date you paid any tax, whichever is later. (If you filed earlier than the due date, it's considered as filed on the due date.)

If you have any complaints about the IRS, call their nearest office to find out where you should write. Two IRS publications which contain a lot of useful information are Publication 910: *Taxpayer's Guide to IRS Information, Assistance, and Publications* and Publication 586A: *The Collection Process (Income Tax Accounts).*

The Audit & Appeals Process

The job the IRS performs year-round in issuing regulations and tax forms, collecting tax returns and payments, auditing the results, and sending out refunds is indeed awesome. Often, the job is done efficiently and rapidly. But some taxpayers have found just the reverse to be true. Repetitive audits, computer breakdowns, demands for taxes not owed, and misinformation are just some of the complaints taxpayers have made about the IRS.

What you need to learn from this is not to feel threatened if you're being audited by the IRS. As long as you're armed with tax knowledge, good

records, and the necessary documentation, you can feel perfectly confident when questioned. The IRS is much less likely to spend audit time on you than on someone with poor records or no records at all.

How returns are selected for audit. Since an average of only 25 out of every 1,000 tax returns are selected each year, most taxpayers never get audited. Don't think that just because you *are* selected you're suspected of being dishonest. Also don't think that because you received your refund you won't be audited. A look at the information below will help explain the selection process:

1. The majority of all selected returns (approximately 75%) come from a computer program called Discriminant Function System (DIF) which attaches a certain score to every line on your return. The computer compares your return with averages of other taxpayers in your tax bracket and attaches a line-by-line score. The higher your score above their predetermined minimum, the more likely you are to be selected.

2. The Taxpayer Compliance Measurement Program (TCMP) is a totally random-sample

selection process. The sample for the entire nation is small (about 50,000), but you might call it the unlucky lottery system. It's a time-consuming examination where you'll be expected to prove *every* item on your return.

3. In the matching documents method, computers match income information supplied to the IRS on forms (such as the W-2 and 1099) with information on taxpayers' returns.

4. Certain target groups, such as designated occupations and tax shelters, are selected from time to time for auditing.

5. Unusual fluctuations or changes in income or expenses could flag your return for audit. Travel and entertainment expenses have always been a popular audit subject.

6. Tips from informants, often ex-spouses or unhappy ex-employees, can trigger an audit.

7. Repetitive audits are legal as long as the previous one resulted in additional tax due. However, if the same items in a previous year resulted in no change in liability, you can probably get the audit suspended.

If your return shows some unusual or large amounts that you feel could target your return for auditing, attach proof for the amounts directly to your return, along with a narrative explanation. Always make sure all income is declared, so there will be no discrepancy between your return and information already supplied to the IRS. Generally, the IRS can audit your returns for the 3 previous years. If fraud is suspected or no return is filed, it can go back to any year.

How to prepare for an audit. The principal reasons the IRS disallows deductions are incomplete records and inadequate substantiation for claimed expenses. Provide the proof and all you'll need is a lot of patience to survive an audit. It also helps if you can communicate using *their* terms and if you understand tax law as much as possible.

You'll have to decide whether to handle the audit yourself or have a qualified professional represent you. If the issues are simple and the amounts involved are small, try it alone. If not, get help (see page 132 for information on how to select a tax advisor). You should, however, compare the potential tax savings with your advisor's estimated fees. When large amounts of tax are at stake, a professional may achieve a quicker resolution and a more favorable one for you as well.

Regardless of who deals with the IRS, here are some suggestions which will be of help:

1. If possible, insist that the entire matter be handled by correspondence and telephone. This allows you to stick to the issues, avoid personality conflicts, and resolve the audit more quickly.

2. If it must be in person, be familiar with your return, especially the items in question. IRS agents are under a lot of pressure to reach an agreement at the first meeting, so use this to your advantage by bringing everything you might possibly need to prove each item.

3. If the item in question is in a gray area, be aggressive, especially if your records are complete. Argue that you're supplying exactly what the law requires.

4. With prior approval, you can tape-record all meetings, and so can the IRS.

5. And now for the don'ts. Don't try to be buddies with the agent or, conversely, get angry. Don't volunteer any information—just answer the questions. Don't sign anything until you've had a lot of time to review it (with professional help), because once you sign a consent form, there's no appeal.

If you and the agent agree, it's over. If you don't, ask to see the agent's supervisor, who may be easier to deal with in trying to reach a final agreement.

The appeals process. The IRS has established an elaborate system of appeals which offers you a wide variety of options. If you didn't reach an agreement with the agent's supervisor, your next stop, and the only one still within the IRS, is the Appeals Office in your region. It's very informal— you can represent yourself if you like—and most audits are resolved at this level. This is because the appeals officer can bargain with you, so be aware that negotiation will be a constant activity from this point forward. There can be good-faith settlement offers and counteroffers on both sides.

The higher the authority, the more likely the compromise—the IRS wants to settle as much as you. For information about this and other related subjects, ask your local IRS office for Publication 556: *Examination of Returns, Appeal Rights, and Claims for Refund.*

Keep in mind that at any stage of the appeal procedure you can do any of the following:

1. Agree and arrange to pay the tax.
2. Ask the IRS to send you a notice of deficiency in order for you to file a petition with the Tax Court.
3. Pay the tax and immediately file a claim for a refund.

The court system. More and more taxpayers are settling disputes with the IRS through litigation. The number of new cases has more than doubled in the past 5 years, resulting in a large backlog.

The Tax Court will only hear your case if the disputed tax has not been assessed or paid. If it has been paid and you've filed for a refund, you must file suit either in the U.S. District Court or the U.S. Court of Claims. You may represent yourself or have an attorney or someone else admitted to practice before that court represent you.

binding decision can be rendered with a minimum of expense and delay, trial judges have much latitude as to the rules of evidence, and the proceedings are simple and informal.

No formal written opinion is issued, and the decision can't be used as a precedent by other taxpayers. But you give up your right to appeal if the decision goes against you. For a petition form and other information, write to the Clerk of the Court, U.S. Tax Court, 400 Second Street, NW, Washington, D.C. 20217. ■

Tax$aver Tip. *If the dispute involves $10,000 or less (including taxes and penalties) for any one tax year, you can have it handled as a "small tax case." The advantages are that you can represent yourself, a final*

Glossary of IRS Terms

Actual cost method (ACM): A method for claiming automobile operating costs that requires the taxpayer to keep detailed records of each item of expense, including depreciation. The total (not including any parking fees and tolls) is multiplied by the percentage of business use applicable to the car.

Adjusted basis: The actual cost of an asset (basis) plus any additions, such as major improvements made, and less any reductions, such as depreciation claimed.

Adjusted gross income (AGI): Gross income from all sources reduced by certain allowable deductions and losses (but not itemized deductions).

Associated with test: Expenses for entertainment are deductible if considered associated with the active conduct of a trade or business; a clear business purpose in making the expenditure must be established, in addition to its being ordinary and necessary.

Basis: The actual cost of an asset.

Business associate: Any person with whom a taxpayer could reasonably expect to engage or deal in the active conduct of a trade or business, such as a customer, client, employee, partner, or professional advisor, whether established or prospective.

Business entertainment: Covers any business-connected activity generally considered to constitute entertainment, as well as recreation and amusement.

Business relationship test: There must be a proximate relationship to business or to business benefits to meet this test.

Business use percentage (BUP): A percentage determined by dividing business use (either in square footage, miles, or time) by total square footage, miles, or time available for all uses.

Capital expenditure: A major addition or improvement to property that is permanent in nature, increases the value or extends the life of the property, and cannot be deducted in the year incurred (it must be depreciated).

Cash basis method: A method of reporting income only when actually received and deducting expenses only when actually paid.

Convenience of employer test: This test is satisfied if an employer requires an employee to use something as a condition of employment in order to properly perform the employee's duties.

Depreciation: The systematic allocation of the cost of an asset over some period of time, either in equal annual amounts, called straight-line, or at various rates, called the accelerated method.

Employee: Someone subject to the will and control of an employer as to what work is done and when it is done.

Exclusive use test: This test is satisfied if the portion of the home being used for business purposes is not used for any other purpose at any time during the taxable year.

Fair market value (FMV): An amount which would influence a willing seller to sell and a willing buyer to buy, each with no pressure to do so.

Gross income: All taxable income except for certain items enumerated and excluded by law.

Improvements: *See* Capital expenditure.

Inventory: Tangible personal property either in the process of being produced or completed and held for sale in the normal course of business.

Involuntary conversion: Property disposed of either by condemnation or by a casualty or theft loss.

Listed property: Depreciable business property used as a means of transportation; any property of a type generally used for purposes of entertainment, recreation, or amusement; and any computer not used exclusively at a regular business establishment.

Ordinary and necessary: An expenditure is *ordinary* if it is a common and accepted practice in a particular trade or business; to be *necessary*, it should be appropriate and helpful in the performance, promotion, or furtherance of a trade or business. *Necessary* does not mean absolutely essential, but it also can't be unreasonable.

Ordinary income: Any income taxed at regular rates and not subject to any preferred tax treatment.

Outside sales: The business of selling and soliciting, away from the employer's place of business, the products or services of the employer.

Placed in service: The date property is in a state of readiness and is available for a specific use.

Points: A term used to describe mortgage charges, usually based on a percentage of the mortgage, paid by the borrower.

Principal place of business: The primary location for conducting business, determined by income earned, time spent, and facilities available there.

Principal residence: The home where the taxpayer resides.

Pro rata: A proportionate division or distribution of income or expenses according to some exactly calculable factor, such as a percentage.

Recapture rule: When tax benefits claimed under certain rules for depreciation and investment tax credit have to be paid back because of something that occurs in a later year, such as an early disposition of the asset or because the business use percentage 50% test is no longer being met.

Repairs: Expenditures to keep property in good condition but which do not increase its value or prolong its useful life.

Residential property: A term that usually refers to a taxpayer's own residence.

S corporation: A corporation whose shareholders have all elected to individually pay tax on their distributive share of corporate income.

Section 179 deduction: An election that allows a taxpayer to write off the entire cost (up to $10,000 beginning in 1987) of an asset the year it's placed in service, subject to income limitations.

Standard mileage rate method (SMR): An optional method for claiming automobile operating costs whereby the total miles driven for business or investment use are multiplied by an IRS-approved rate (currently 21¢ per mile for the first 15,000 miles). A rate of 11¢ per mile applies for additional mileage and for fully depreciated cars. A standard rate of 9¢ per mile applies to mileage for moving purposes; 12¢ per mile to mileage for charitable purposes.

Tax preparer: Any person who prepares income tax returns for compensation, or who employs others to do so. Preparing a return means obtaining information, determining which tax rules apply and how they should be applied, computing the tax, and completing the forms.

Trade or business: Any activity carried on for livelihood or for profit and where there is some type of economic activity involved. It is characterized by the regularity of such activities and transactions and by the production of income.

Useful life: The expected reasonable number of years that an asset is used in a trade or business or for the production of income. ■

Index